Jim Wynn's Recomm
for the River W

Dedicated to
Jim Wynn
and
Professor Tom Cross

The River Wharfe, Farfield Hall

NORTH COUNTRY FLY PATTERNS

Jim Wynn's Recommended Flies for the River Wharfe

Martin Cross

MCP

2011

Published by MCP
7 Riverside Close, Otley, West Yorkshire LS21 2RN

© Martin Cross, 2011
www.martincrosspublishing.co.uk
ISBN 978 0 9567400 0 7

Book design: Richard Reeve
Cover photograph: River Wharfe, Farfield Hall,
near Addingham, West Yorkshire (Martin Cross)
Photographs of flies: Peter Hendry LMPA, LEIPP
Photographs of the River Wharfe: Martin Cross
Printed in the UK

Contents

About the author

Dr. Martin Cross was born in Nottingham in 1958; he is married to Linda and they have three children Joe, Robbie and Tom. Martin has lived in Otley, West Yorkshire for most of his life. He attended Prince Henry's Grammar School, Otley. Since gaining his doctorate in Engineering Geology from the University of Nottingham he has worked as a consultant engineer for over 25 years specialising in engineering geology, geotechnical engineering and geo-environmental engineering. He is a Chartered Scientist, Environmentalist, Geologist and Engineer.

Martin was taught to fish by his late father Professor Tom Cross. He has been a member of the Otley Angling Club since 1969 and has regulary fished the club's waters since this date. He is also a member of the Bradford Waltonians Angling Club and regularly fishes the River Wharfe at Denton near Ilkley. He has attended the fly tying courses run by Stephen Cheetham, the North Country pattern specialist at Prince Henry's Grammar School, Otley. Martin regularly fishes the Pool, Otley, Denton, Appletreewick, Bolton Abbey and Burnsall sections of the River Wharfe. On occasions he also fishes the Ure, Nidd and Swale. He also fishes the Rivers Lune and Ribble in Lancashire, the Dovey and Teifi in Wales and the Boarder Esk, Nith and Spey in Scotland.

Foreword

by Leslie Magee, Pool in Wharfedale, 1992

Jim Wynn (1898-1974) lived at 49 Southfield Terrace, Addingham, and in the 1940s had acquaintances among the Otley School of fly-tyers who were prominent during the second half of the last century and first quarter of this. He was well known to Tom Chippendale (1877-1957), the professional fly-tyer and inventor who lived in Otley.

William Brumfitt (1846-1926) was the most outstanding fly-fisher and fly-tyer of his day on the Wharfe. He tied and supplied most of the patterns for Pritt's *Yorkshire Trout Flies* and eventually passed on his manuscript book of patterns and dressings, illustrated with fine, actual size water colours to Tom Chippendale who continued to add new patterns and water colour paintings of flies together with the hook sizes and dressings. Many of the additions were dry flies based on the Halford series, a feature being the use of Andalusian cock hackles. In addition, there were loch or lake flies as well as patterns published in the *Fishing Gazette* and the originator of the flies is always given. I have a computer programme which enables me to compare new lists with older lists quite rapidly and this indicates that Wynn's patterns are based on Halford's, possibly from Chippendale's instructions but with the substitution of synthetic fibres which became available from around 1939.

The Orange Tag is a Halford pattern and is in fact the fly often called the Treacle Parkin, although there is a tendency of modern writers to give it a yellow tag. There is now evidence that such a fly was a Wharfedale creation. However, J. W. Sagar of Ilkley quotes the Orange Tag in a 1915 appendix to Swarbrick's manuscript list of 1807, but he makes no claim to it being any other than Halford's.

Jim Wynn was concerned earlier with the 'exact' representation of insects and published some excellent patterns in the old *Fishing Gazette* around 1942-1943 (see later). A friend, who is a great collector of all to do with North Country Style fishing tradition, gave me details of the tyings which he took from the *Fishing Gazette* when he was at school on the Eden during the Second World War. Two of these, the Water Cricket and the Green Olive, I regularly use on hot days and summer evenings.

Jim Wynn was among those who first used and adapted the chalk stream patterns of southern England for use on northern rivers, following the lead of Francis Walbran, who first saw them used on the Ure by his guest, W. Senior. Walbran wrote with great enthusiasm about the new style and he was followed by Chippendale, Edmonds and Lee, Wynn and many others who saw an alternative to spinning, dapping with the live fly (bobbing) and the upstream worm. Of course, one of the advantages of Wynn's patterns is that many of them may be used wet or dry as the circumstances dictate. The development and use of the dry fly combined with the use of the traditional wet flies has removed much of the frustration of our North Country fly fishing suffered by the Victorians.

The mayfly which occurs on Chelker Reservoir is *Ephemera Vulgata* (the Dark Mackerel of Ronalds). It is confined in Yorkshire to Winterburn reservoir, the Washburn Valley reservoirs and the Leeds-Liverpool Canal from the Lancashire border to the centre of Leeds. The Dark Mackerel pattern was reported by Jim Wynn as a pattern 'which will kill at every cast'; such patterns should be banned forthwith!

Jim Wynn's list of flies is an interesting historical document well worthy of preservation.

Preface

This book documents a collection of wet and dry fly dressings for the River Wharfe, as recorded by Jim Wynn in two notebooks, and sets them in the context of Wharfedale and the tradition of the North Country style of fly-fishing. The notebooks were discovered in 1991, seventeen years after Jim Wynn's death. Some of the flies are modifications of traditional North Country patterns, others were his own creations, but almost all show the introduction of coloured tinsels and man-made fibres which was an innovation fifty years ago.

Jim Wynn was the river keeper of the Bradford Waltonians Angling Club's Farfield Hall stretch of the River Wharfe near Bolton Abbey, North Yorkshire. As keeper he knew this stretch of the Wharfe intimately. Jim Wynn was an expert angler and fly-tyer and, above all, dressed flies that would catch fish.

This book is dedicated firstly to Jim Wynn and secondly to my late father Professor Tom Cross, an Otley resident and member of the Bradford Waltonians Angling Club, who carefully documented the information contained in the two little red notebooks, one containing dry fly dressings and the other containing wet fly dressings. A pamphlet entitled *Jim Wynn's Recommended Flies For The River Wharfe*, edited by Tom Cross, was produced for Bradford Waltonian Angling Club members in February 1992. Tom Cross was also responsible for providing some of the original editorial comments on Jim Wynn's dressings. This book draws on, develops, and greatly expands upon the information contained in this pamphlet. The same Foreword provided by Leslie Magee which appeared in the pamphlet is included in this book. The chapter on Jim Wynn is also taken from this pamphlet.

The author would like to acknowledge the assistance of members of the Bradford Waltonians Angling Club who contributed to the original pamphlet, especially G. B. Lowe (Bradford), the late E. H. Wright (Hawksworth), D. Crutch (Silsden), C. K. E. Pearson (Cross Hills), J. M. Padgett (Guiseley) and late J. H. Eastwood (Silsden).

Thanks are also extended to Leslie Magee (Pool-in-Wharfedale), author of *Fly Fishing: The North Country Tradition*, for his Foreword and Peter Lowndes (Kirby Overblow) for very helpful discussions and their help in providing cuttings from the *Fishing Gazette*.

Thanks go to members of the Bradford Waltonians Angling Club and other friends and acquaintances who have read and made comments on the manuscript, including Professor Michael Gardener, Professor Richard Peace, Professor David Ramsden, Mr Michael Padgett (Orvis), Mr Stephen Cheetham (Fishing With Style, Yeadon) and Mr Steve Bielby (Wharfedale Angling Classics, Otley).

One interesting discovery during the attempt to trace Jim Wynn's patterns and record the dressings was to realise how many of his flies still exist in the fly boxes of members of the Waltonians Angling Club. Original examples of the Chelker Greenwell were supplied by Michael Padgett and Eric Wright and the former even had a small wallet holding several casts complete with Jim Wynn-dressed flies that had been used by Willie Hanson at Chelker just before his death. Michael Padgett also had several examples of the Great Red Sedge. David Crutch produced a box of beautifully tied wet and dry flies together with a bulging leather wallet containing hundreds of examples of Jim Wynn's flies in small neatly labelled packets. Truly a collector's item!

I would like to give special thanks to Mike Reed of Island Flies, Isle of Lewis who expertly tied all the flies for this book and Peter Hendry (LMPA, LBIPP), a professional photographer from Otley who photographed them so that the dressings can be copied to match those shown. Mike's comments on tying each fly have been added to the comments section succeeding Jim Wynn's description of each fly dressing. Taking good photographs of small North Country fly patterns is not a simple task and Peter demonstrated great ingenuity in setting up the equipment to take the photographs. The fly images have been enlarged to assist the fly-tyer.

I am also very grateful for the helpful assistance of Richard Reeve for the design of the book.

Introduction

Inventing a new artificial fly for trout and grayling is relatively simple when one considers the possible permutations of the multitudes of feathers, furs, silks, fibres and man-made materials now available. Examples can be found each month in the angling press and are often labelled with eye-catching names such as Zed's Zonker or Uniquely Ure(s)!

Describing a new fly which will deceive fish regularly is much more difficult and usually demands considerable experience as a naturalist, fly-tyer and angler. The general acceptance of a new pattern can take many years of field trials, publicity, marketing and sales. Flies that have evolved through this process for the rivers in a local area of the country are very useful because they reduce some of the problems facing newcomers wishing to fish an unfamiliar river. The newcomer can concentrate more on fly presentation and timing, having confidence in the tackle and flies they are using.

Anglers on Yorkshire's River Wharfe are especially fortunate in having so many excellent flies available to them from the experience and publications of angling fly-dressers who practised during the past two centuries. The majority of these North Country fly patterns are wet flies, but it is now possible to widen the spectrum and angling methods by revealing the dressings of a series of dry flies that were devised or selected and modified by Jim Wynn, a river keeper, enthusiastic angler and expert fly-tyer, who knew the River Wharfe intimately. He was one of the earliest anglers to evaluate and use the variety of tinsels and man-made fibres being appraised and then utilized for weaving decorative fabrics in the 1930s.

Jim Wynn's dry fly patterns were first noticed towards the end of 1991 in a small red notebook that had been the property of an unapprised angler for several years. Subsequent enquiries uncovered a second notebook containing Jim Wynn's wet fly patterns and many examples of flies that he had dressed.

This book attempts to give some background information on Jim Wynn, to record his dressings, and add his suggestions on when to use the pattern. The book includes thirty-four dry fly dressings and forty-nine wet fly dressings. The details of the dressings of each fly, together with comments on the use of the fly are those provided by Jim Wynn in his little red notebooks. It is emphasised that this text is unaltered and in the exact format as recorded by Jim Wynn in his notebooks.

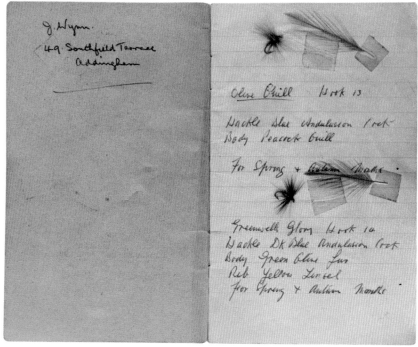

Jim Wynn's original notebook of dry fly patterns.

Further observations and comments about each fly have been included as bullet points. These comments are largely those of the author and the late Professor Tom Cross, the author's father, who in particular provided specific comments on the appearance of the fly dressings and the sample hackles included in the notebooks. The bulleted comments also include observations and information about the historical development of the flies; this information has been drawn from a wide range of angling literature referenced at the end of the book.

As it was not possible to photograph the original Jim Wynn fly-dressings included in the notebooks, all the flies in this book have been expertly tied by Mike Reed of Island Flies, Isle of Lewis. Mike Reed had obtained a copy of the original pamphlet, *Jim Wynn's Recommended Flies for the River Wharfe* and had been tying Jim's dressings professionally for a number of years for Angling and Country Sports, a shop located at Cross Green in Otley. As Mike has first hand experience in tying the flies, his comments are also included at the end of the bulleted comments section which it is hoped will assist the fly-tyer. Mike says: 'There was an instant appeal in tying these flies. Patterns that have been tied in the past have an element of time travel about them. No surprise that others have passed this way before but always a comfort. The minute I started making these flies it became obvious that Jim Wynn had a distinct style towards tying. This I suspect coloured all elements of his life. He would have been an interesting chap to have a pint with.'

This book extends the original pamphlet with a new section which aims to give background and context to the development and use of Jim Wynn's fly patterns. The course of the River Wharfe is described from its source, through Upper, Middle and Lower Wharfedale to its confluence with the River Ouse, exploring the natural history of the river and geology of the surrounding landscape. The North Country tradition of wet fly fishing and the development of North Country patterns is introduced and a survey of some of the noteable fisherman who fished the River Wharfe is included. It will become obvious that Jim Wynn should be placed in the line of outstanding North Country anglers and fly-dressers who have been associated with the River Wharfe and neighbouring Yorkshire rivers.

A list of key manuscripts and fly-lists relevant to the River Wharfe is included in the references. Appendix 1 presents a table of mayflies (upwinged flies) for the River Wharfe together with the common angling name of the fly and the corresponding Jim Wynn pattern. In order to assist the fly-fisherman to select the appropriate dressings in relation to the flies present on the River Wharfe during the season, Appendix 2 provides a seasonal calendar of Jim Wynn's dry flies and Appendix 3 a seasonal calendar of Jim Wynn's wet flies. The seasonal calendars also indicate dressings which Jim Wynn suggested can be used for grayling, dressings suitable for use in the evening and dressings which can be used following a spate. Appendix 4 separately lists Jim Wynn's recommendations of fly-dressings suitable for grayling fishing.

Part One

*An expanded and illustrated
version of an original pamphlet
produced in 1992 by Tom Cross for
the Bradford Waltonians Angling Club*

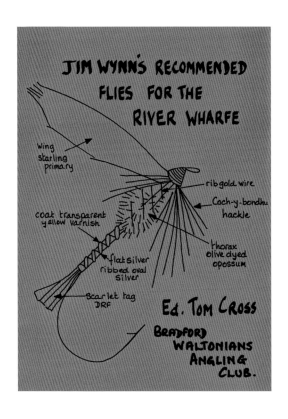

Jim Wynn of Addingham – a leading Yorkshire fly-tyer (1951)

Jim Wynn, fly-tyer

Jim Wynn (1898-1974) loved the River Wharfe and, in particular, the Farfield Hall area of the river located below Kex Beck and upstream of Addingham*. This beautiful stretch of the river, containing one reach aptly named Paradise Lathe (shown on the front cover) and overlooked by the friendly but imposing summit of Beamsley Beacon, has a succession of deep pools, shingle runs dotted with boulders and slow glides overhung with trees; ideal fly-fishing water for trout and grayling. It also contains interesting sections suitable for upstream worming and deep water in the heavily wooded lower length for trotting a variety of baits.

Jim Wynn served in the Guards during the First World War and sustained a leg injury which left him with a permanent limp. He returned to live in Addingham and became a fly-fishing enthusiast (some would even say a fanatic). He was retained as part-time river keeper on the Farfield Hall estate and became full-time river keeper for the Bradford Waltonians Angling Club, when the Club leased this stretch of the River Wharfe. Most days during the spring, summer and autumn months of his later years were spent by the river and no angling club could wish for a more conscientious keeper. His years of experience on Yorkshire rivers enabled him to give anglers valuable advice on where and when to fish, and what flies to use. Fishing trips with past members of the Bradford Waltonians Angling Club (especially Willie Hanson) to rivers such as the Eamont, Eden, Border Esk, Annan and Findhorn widened his horizons and allowed him to experiment further. He was an expert fly-dresser and always carried a tin of his creations, from which he would proffer selected examples to members of the Club, who he believed needed and would appreciate help.

When Jim died on 15 September 1974 at the age of 76, the disciples of Walton lost a very perceptive and likeable man, and a fly-tying artist. Many of the older Bradford Waltonians Angling Club members benefited from his help. It is hoped that this publication will help disseminate his knowledge and expertise to other anglers who already fish or wish to fish the River Wharfe.

Jim compiled a handwritten list of his selected dry flies and their dressings in a red-covered notebook, together with an example of each fly and a specimen hackle. This little red book was given to Waltonian Charlie Sharpe

* National Grid Ref. 4077 4517

Jim Wynn waiting patiently for his hot bacon sandwich during a fishing trip to the River Eamont in 1968.

(now deceased) and eventually became the property of Berry Lowe, a current member of the Club. The thirty-two patterns described in this unique 'little red book' are now given exactly as written, together with Jim Wynn's suggestions on when they should be used.

Another red notebook containing Jim Wynn's wet fly dressings was subsequently discovered by Waltonian David Crutch, and this contained some fascinating examples of novel dressings and Jim's helpful comments.

Jim Wynn's wet fly patterns, as contained in the second little red book, appear to have been prepared for T. K. Wilson of Skipton. The late T. K. Wilson (Timmy Wilson) was a well known angler and writer who wrote under the pseudonym of Broughton Point for the *Dalesman* magazine and *Yorkshire Post* newspaper. It is possible that Jim Wynn sent the wet fly dressings for inclusion in one of his regular angling articles within the *Dalesman* or *Yorkshire Post*. It now seems unlikely that Timmy Wilson received this correspondence before he died in 1965.

In a covering letter addressed to T. K. Wilson, Jim Wynn introduced the wet fly dressings in the little red book as follows:

Forty-odd dressings of flies written from memories of good days on Yorkshire rivers. There are others of course but the dressings given should see one through the season on any North Country trout stream.

The killing power of any fly is due to the method of dressing. Any old feather won't do; if a fly isn't worth a good hackle then it isn't worth making.

The 'Mongrel Tups' (A Yorkshire Tie of Tups) may come in for some questioning but the fact remains that it is experience that counts. There are a lot of reflections from tinsels and bright acetate varnished bodies, as for example in the Mongrel Tups where the yellow converges to the pink which converges to the hackle. We get a good combination of colours that will be seen by the trout against the background of all the colours of nature.

The changes in the bodies, I think, is not wholly due to their casting a sheath. I am certain most of them are due to them feeding on the vegetation. A fly newly hatched out can, in a short time, be a different colour altogether.

The object of fishing three flies on a wet cast is that on one part of the river they may be taking a certain fly yet a hundred yards further along they may be taking a different fly altogether.

What can be better sport than fishing a team of flies upstream? What is there in sitting on the bank with a pint of maggots? It is a sport for the over-eighties when old age creeps in and they're no longer able to wade a stream. The bait fishers don't know what they are missing; it is sheer idleness besides being a lot of bother in taking a pannier full of all kinds of tackle – most of which are never used.

They use, also, about 90 per cent of maggots for ground-bait and 10 per cent for the hook. What do they achieve? They have some sport granted, but they ram disgorgers into undersized fish and throw them back anyhow. What sizeable fish they get are chock-full of maggots and who wants to give a friend a trout with maggots crawling of its mouth anyway. We have plenty of pollution without throwing gallons of maggots into the stream; if they are not taken by young fish they are left on the bottom to go sour.

We know that Jim Wynn kept other notebooks of dressings recommended by earlier Wharfe anglers and fly-tyers such as Abraham Wilkinson (1842) of Leeds, William Brumfitt, William Robinson, Timothy Thackeray and Joshua Hart (1846-1908) of Otley, Michael Theakston (1853) of Ripon, Pritt (1885, 1886) of Leeds, Sylvester Lister (1898) of Bolton Abbey, Joseph Emmott (1900) of Ilkley and Edmonds and Lee (1916) of Leeds. However, these present compilations would appear to be the collection of flies he used and recommended for the River Wharfe. It is likely that he borrowed patterns and ideas from earlier publications and lists, but many are his own versions and creations (see list of manuscripts, page 137).

Jim Wynn was an innovator. He attempted to evaluate and incorporate into his fly-dressings, man-made fibres and decorative threads being introduced into the textile industry. This practice was rather frowned upon by the purist fly-tyer at that time, but is now common practice. Consequently, the reader will soon realise that many of the dressings are rather unconventional and some comments have been added by the author, where appropriate, to relate the name and dressing to the pattern published in recognised reference books. The author has also included information on what the pattern imitates and when to fish the fly. Seasonal calendars for both dry and wet fly patterns are also included in the Appendices.

The fly-patterns in Jim Wynn's little red books are his recommended flies for use on the River Wharfe. The patterns are reproduced in this book in order to encourage anglers to continue to fish for trout with the fly on the River Wharfe and hopefully to try their hand to dress their own flies. The original pamphlet was dedicated to the memory of Jim Wynn who was devoted to the Bradford Waltonians Angling Club and the River Wharfe. I suspect that one might sense his presence on the banks of the River Wharfe at Farfield Hall, watching over his trout and grayling and keeping an eye open for poachers.

General tying notes

Some of the hook sizes recommended by Jim Wynn are odd numbers, and now, virtually unobtainable. Certain 'tinsels' (e.g. yellow, pink and orange) and fluorescent threads specified by Jim Wynn were probably obtained as scraps from John Knox's textile firm in Silsden, where he had worked as a weft man and which manufactured a range of fancy decorated cloths and fabrics. The use of these materials illustrates Jim's imagination and inventiveness, but obviously makes it difficult for others to reproduce an exact copy; perhaps some of the currently available fibres and shades of Lurex or Mylar might provide a suitable alternative. Substitute materials are provided for dressings where required.

Several of the dry fly patterns have a 'double hackle'. The hackle towards the hook bend is termed 'legs' and the conventional shoulder hackle is towards the eye. All the dry fly patterns lack wings, but specify cock hackles, and the examples provided are dressed fairly full with at least three to four turns. The dry-fly dressings in the red notebook would ensure buoyancy when fished upstream in broken water and would also aid visibility. Wet fly versions can be prepared by substituting hen hackles, and they would complement the excellent wet fly patterns for the River Wharfe after Pritt (1885, 1886) or by

Edmonds and Lee (1916) and also by Jim Wynn in the *Fishing Gazette* (1943) or contained in the second Little Red Book (see later).

A head of peacock, magpie or ostrich herl was a common feature in the earlier wet fly dressings tied on hooks whipped directly onto gut. With the introduction of eyed hooks this practice was largely discontinued in the belief that the metal eye plus the tying silk gave the necessary shape to the artificial. Jim Wynn retained a herl head on some of his patterns and also believed that an additional loop of orange or red tinsel at the head supplied the iridescence of insect eyes which had been lost in the modified dressings. It would be interesting to carry out a controlled comparison of flies with and without this added feature.

Several of Jim Wynn's fly patterns included feathers from birds which are now protected and even very rare (e.g. the dotterel, water rail and corncrake). Anglers *must not* attempt to obtain wings or skins of protected birds unless they have been recovered from the roadside after being hit by a car or lorry, but such corpses are more likely to be blackbirds or starlings. One must remember that Wharfedale gamekeepers used to kill the merlin, sparrowhawk and harrier on sight and display them on their gibbets along with moles and red squirrels. Thankfully, those unenlightened days have now passed but it does mean that certain fly patterns cannot be faithfully reproduced and we shall have to experiment with substitute feathers.

Comments from Mike Reed

Wherever possible I have used the materials Jim Wynn did. On occasion I have used modern substitutes. Jim Wynn dressed his flies using the materials he found around him, either at work, on the river bank, or at his home. I do the same for many of my tyings and used the same method when substituting materials here. I would like to think he would approve.

The flies photographed in this book were tied on the only English made hooks there are now, Sprite of Redditch. They have an old fashioned look to them that suits the style of North Country patterns well. Most of the dry flies were tied on up-eye size 14 hooks and wet flies on down-eye sizes 14 and 16 hooks apart from the larger mayfly and sedge patterns. All silks and most materials were supplied by E. Veniard; no doubt Jim Wynn would have used the same.

When finished, the flies make an interesting set of North Country dressings. No doubt the intrepid fly-tyer may well be able to find some of the materials that I had to substitute. Whenever I did use alternatives I tried to keep in the spirit of Jim Wynn's fly-tying ethos; varnish, floss and tinsels were all part of that, along with a practical mind that used what he found on the floor, not a bad idea!

Wet fly patterns

* Published in the *Fishing Gazette*.

Small Ant Fly

Very useful when there is a flight of ants which sometimes fall on the water and also if there happens to be an ants nest located near the water edge which is submerged by a rise in river level. It is also a good grayling fly.

HOOK: 15

HACKLE: A red-bronze feather from the back of a fieldfare, one turn of hackle is enough.

BODY: Orange tinsel with a fairly large blob of orange transparent varnish at the tail and one at the thorax.

HEAD: Orange tinsel and a turn of bronze peacock herl.

Comments

• Red ant (*Hymenoptera rubra*). The red ant grows wings during the mating season and become airborne, usually on hot humid days in July and August. This insect is very abundant on the water after a swarm or flight of ants. However, it should be appreciated that this takes place only one or two days a year, lucky is the angler who is present at the waterside on one of these days. Providing the angler has a matching imitation he is assured of a memorable day's fishing.

Mike Reed's comments: Use varnished soaked fluo orange Uni floss for the body and substitute the fieldfare hackle with a reddy brown hackle outer covert feather from a woodcock wing. The head is a single turn of herl taken from the peacock eye, plus a turn of floss.

Green and Yellow Bloa

One of the light duns and may be taken as an imitation of the Yellow Sally. It is without doubt a useful fly during the summer months.

HOOK: 14 and 16

HACKLE: The whitish feather from the hooded crow neck.

BODY: Olive green and yellow silks twisted together and wrapped in alternate bands, then ribbed with fine gold tinsel.

Comments
- Probably taken as a pale watery dun *(Baetis fuscatus)* or possibly a yellow may dun *(Heptagenia sulphurea)*. Emergence during the day and early evening throughout the summer.
- Also possibly taken as a small yellow sally stonefly *(Chloroperla torrentium)*. Found in all types of water with stony sub-strata. Appears mainly in April to June and sometimes to August.

Mike Reed's comments: The hooded crow is a protected bird species; we have lots of them in the Hebrides. At some point I will find a dead one and be able to tie this with the actual feather. In the meantime, substitute a white/grey hen hackle.

Blue Dun Hackle
(Yorkshire Tie of the Devonshire Blue Upright)

This is quite a good fly in spring and should be given a trial when the angler is in doubt as what to put on next after a day of wondering what they are taking; may save a blank day.

HOOK: 14

HACKLE: Blue dun hackle, dark, from outside the coot wing.

BODY: Gun-metal artificial silk ribbed with fine silver tinsel.

HEAD: Gun-metal silk.

Comments
- Iron blue dun *(Baetis niger* and *B. muticus)*. Also good general pattern for smaller olives. Emergence at the surface in open water throughout the summer, with peaks in May and September.
- This fly is associated with R. S. Austin who was responsible for the well-known West Country pattern. Austin tied the fly with cream silk.
- As a grayling fly the Blue Upright is a great favourite with many anglers and is generally fished wet as a bob fly.

Mike Reed's comments: The gunmetal silk was the challenge here. I dyed white gossamer silk grey/black and waxed it well to achieve a pleasing effect. The body is ribbed with tinsel; to my eyes, wire suits the fly better, and I'm not sure what JW means by tinsel.

Blue Hen Spider

HOOK: 14

HACKLE: Blue dun hen – dun meaning
dull greyish-brown colour.

BODY: Rear half olive Lurex; thorax,
mole fur ribbed with olive Lurex.

Comments

• This wet fly dressing by JW and termed one of his 'specials' did not appear in his
notebook but was recorded by Keith Pearson (Bradford Waltonians).

• The Blue Dun Spider provides a good general nymph pattern but it will also imitate
any of the olives since both the shade of the hackle and body dubbing may be varied
from light to dark. Thus the angler may move through the whole spectrum from
pale watery olives to dark olives or even the iron blue dun. This is another pattern
which reveals the time honoured skill of blending colours of silk or fur to produce the
required shade. Since the time of Charles Cotton there have been many versions of
the Blue Dun.

Mike Reed's comments: Varnished olive floss for the body and rib.

Yellow Coot

This is a very good fly to have on with the Waterhen Bloa. May be taken for
the hatching nymph, or on the other hand it is a good imitation of the small
blue midge or dun that appears in spring and autumn. It is a pattern of my
own invention and quite a reliable one to have on the cast in March and April
or in September and October for the grayling. The feather from outside a
merlin hawk wing may be used as a substitute for the coot feather.

HOOK: 15

HACKLE: Small feather from under a
coot wing, again from the bottom row
of feathers.

BODY: Two-thirds blue fox rabbit, a blue
dun shade. The remainder of body – yellow
artificial silk ribbed with fine gold tinsel,
giving a sort of yellow tip to the body.

HEAD: Yellow silk.

Mike Reed's comments: Standard dressing.

Little Pheasant Tail

HOOK: 14 or 16.

HACKLE: Brown partridge, very sparse.

BUTT: Gold Lurex.

THORAX: Lumpy, cross-wound, pheasant tail herl.

This wet fly dressing by Jim Wynn, and termed one of his 'specials', did not appear in his notebook but was recorded by Keith Pearson (Bradford Waltonians).

Comments

• The Little Pheasant Tail is a general pattern tied to resemble darker coloured agile darter nymph species such as the dark olive nymph (*Baetis atrebatinus*, *B. rhodani*) or medium olive nymph (*Baetis Tenax*, *B. vernus*).

• Can be used throughout the season; one to use when there is no hatch or fall of flies and fish are feeding below the surface.

Mike Reed's comments: Standard tying.

Quill Bodied Coot

This is the medium olive fly. Alternatively, a body may be made of blue opossum fur dyed in a yellow dye to give a green-olive fur for dubbing. Rib with fine gold wire. It then becomes of course a type of hackled Greenwell, a very good killer in April and again in autumn for grayling.

HOOK: 14

HACKLE: Small spoon shaped feather from the lower row under a coot wing.

BODY: A large feather outside the coot wing stripped and dyed in yellow dye. This quill when stripped shows white and dark inky blue. When dyed the white shows yellow and inky blue shows green-olive.

Comments

• Medium olive dun (*Baetis tenax*). Emergence during the day or early evening throughout the summer, with a peak in May and June.

Mike Reed's comments: A really nice tying. As for the quill used for the body, does Jim mean the centre quill of the feather dyed and cut to size, or the actual fibres off the quill? You choose!

Yellow Dotterel

When tied with orange silk and hackled with an underwing feather then one has a good resemblance to the light needle. The dotterel is now very scarce in this country and fly men who possess a few feathers are indeed fortunate. Several feathers can be used as a substitute for the dotterel: one of the best is from the hen harrier, one is from a yellow plover second; a young starling underwing feather is of no use whatever. The hooded crow hackle is a very good substitute but lacks the fawnish tips. *[Pritt states that a feather from a young curlew will be found equally attractive].*

HOOK: 14

HACKLE: Feather from outside the dotterel wing which is tipped with a fawnish shade as in the natural fly.

BODY: Straw coloured silk ribbed with fine gold tinsel.

HEAD: Straw coloured silk.

Comments

• Pattern probably tied to resemble a pale watery dun (*Baetis fuscatus bioculatus*) or pale evening dun (*Procloeon bifidum pseudorufulorum*).

• This fly may be an adaptation of Hofland's (1839) The Dotteril Hackle. Hofland's praise of the 'Dotteril Fly' led to the downfall of the dotterel as a breeding species, and by 1904 it was extinct as a breeding bird in the north of England.

• Leslie Magee (1994) suggests a substitute feather from under a woodcock's wing is a close match to the dotterel feather; some starling feathers with gold tips are a close match too (not the underwing).

• T. C. Hofland (1839), William Brumfitt (1845-1926) and Tom Chippendale (1877-1954) tied the hackle 'umbrella' style, by which the hackle must be set by various positions by taking one or two turns of silk round the base of the hackle when finishing off the head (Magee, 1994).

• This fly is also known as the Dotterel Dun. Not only is the Dotterel Dun an excellent nymph pattern but also a fair fly to imitate any of the paler olives in their various stages.

• G. E. M. Skues used this pattern extensively. He tied this pattern as follows. Hook: 18, 16 or 14. Tying thread: pale yellow silk. Hackle: a lightish mottled starling feather with a brownish tinge to it (such feathers are mainly located on the underside of the wing; golden plover hackles are also used). Body: pale yellow silk very lightly dubbed with light hare's ear fur. Dub a little more heavily behind the hackle to form a thorax.

• Oliver Edwards recommends this fly for grayling on the Wharfe from October to November when the pale wateries can be seen. Edwards' pattern included: straw coloured gossamer silk for the body. Starling under covert feather, preferably white/ silver marginal feather.

Mike Reed's comments: Use the inner wing under covert feather from a woodcock wing – it is fawny white and looks good on this fly.

February Red

Very good in the early months. A feather from outside a grouse wing, the dark feather that is spotted at the tips with the fawnish shade, will kill and the fly is then known as the Grouse and Red with the body made of red tinsel in place of the claret dubbed body. Some anglers prefer this second dressing and it is well to have both dressings on the cast and let them have a go before deciding which particular fly to use in the spring.

HOOK: 15

HACKLE: The dark feather from under a woodcock wing which is tipped a light fawnish shade.

BODY: Claret red artificial silk dubbed onto orange silk then ribbed with gold tinsel.

HEAD: Claret tying silk and a turn of peacock herl, for the eyes a loop of red tinsel.

Comments

• This pattern has its roots in one of Alfred Ronalds' dressings which Roger Fogg updated.

• The pattern imitates a small brown stonefly (*Taeniopteryx nebulosa*). Roger Fogg recommends it as an early season pattern (February to April) and has caught larger fish when used with more popular patterns, such as the Partridge and Orange.

• Also imitates *Brachyptera risi*, found on slow flowing stony rivers from March to July.

• It is recommended as a top dropper of a three-fly cast fished up stream.

Mike Reed's comments: Silk dubbed onto silk? I took some claret red silk and frayed it with my finger nails. Do this for a while, breaking the linear fibres, and you end up with some silk dubbing. Use Uni Micro Tinsel for the loop eyes.

Smoke Fly

When the house flies are numbed with cold and get blown onto the river, then the above artificial kills exceedingly well and must not be neglected. It is also a good grayling pattern when a ribbing of gold wire and a red head proves very attractive.

HOOK: 14

HACKLE: A young grouse poult hackle from under the wing.

BODY: Red bronze peacock herl.

HEAD: Orange tinsel.

Comments

• Pattern tied to imitate a Buzzer (*Chironomidae*).

• The Smoke Fly or Shade Fly was included in Sylvester Lister's *List of Flies for the Wharfe* (1889). Lister's pattern was as follows. Feather: dusky white from Norwegian crow (hooded crow) or poult's underwing. Head: magpie herl. Body: purple peacock all the way down. Lister said the fly may be used throughout the season particularly on bright days; when ribbed with silver twist, it is called the Silver Smoke Fly. Excellent for grayling.

• The Smoke Fly is included in T. E. Pritt's *North Country Flies* (1885). Pritt remarked that it was a 'more or less fancy fly, and will only kill in certain curious states of the weather and water. On sluggish water, in dull, heavy, sultry weather, it is sometimes useful.'

• A modern tie of the Smoke Fly is the Griffith's Gnat, however, this is used as an all purpose dry fly. JW tied this as a wet fly to be fished in the surface film. It works best in small sizes (14, 16 and 18) where it suggests all sorts of small insects trapped in the surface film. The Griffith's Gnat uses a grizzle cock hackle. Griffith's said the hackle should be short, with fibre length little more than the gape of the hook.

Mike Reed's comments: Green peacock herl will go bronze if you leave it in the sun for a few days.

Gravel Bed Spider

There are all kinds of attempts at making this spider and all bear some resemblance, especially The Old Master which was dressed by the old Otley fly-tyer Bradley. Sagars Fancy was another in spite of what they say about it being an imitation of the grannom; Sagars Fancy doesn't in any way resemble the grannom fly. The above dressing was originated by a certain

Jim Whittaker, Fish Watcher at Bolton Abbey in the early 1880s and to this day is one of merit. Remember that it is a spider and not a fly.

HOOK: 14

HACKLE: A couple of turns of a feather from a wild drake; a finely spotted feather.

BODY: Lead coloured silk.

HEAD: Peacock herl.

Comments

• Gravel bed (*Hexatoma fuscipennis*), member of the flat-winged *Diptera* order; resembles a miniature crane fly.

• This terrestrial lives in its pupal state in gravel or sand-beds at the edges of rivers. There closeness to the water inevitably means that some of the adults end up on the river, and they can often be seen swarming over the surface.

• Its body is brownish-grey with two heavily veined brownish wings.

• It appears on warm days from late April until early June.

Mike Reed's comments: The lead silk body was made by dying white silk grey/black and then waxing. The speckled drake hackle came from the duck's head/upper breast; use just the tip if you only have larger feathers.

Greensleaves

This fly is easily recognised as the golden eyed gauze wing. Some tiers use a feather from the underwing of a woodcock as the hackle, but the white partridge feather is far better, as its whiteness is also essential in this brilliant coloured fly. There are two sizes of natural fly, large and small; the larger fly is often found miles away from the river. It is blessed with very large wings which are powerful in flight. The above dressing is very good indeed, the green tinsel body proving very attractive.

HOOK: 14

HACKLE: A white, finely speckled feather from under a partridge wing.

BODY: Bright green tinsel coated in clear varnish.

HEAD: Green tinsel with a loop of orange tinsel to represent the very bright eyes.

Comments

- Greensleaves [sic] is normally spelt Green Sleeves (Pritt, 1886). However, did JW purposely spell it as Greensleaves; sleaves is a term used for 'a fine filament that can be separated from a silk fibre, to separate as threads, used in the term sleaved silk, floss silk.' Perhaps this was a quirk based on his knowledge of the vocabulary used in the textile industry.
- This particular pattern was an adaptation of one of Alfred Ronalds' (1836) patterns for the golden eyed gauze wing. According to Ronalds the golden eyed gauze wing is rather a scarce insect upon some waters, but where it is found affords great sport on windy days. Both larger and smaller individuals than that represented by this green sort are to be found, and also a brown kind much larger and with dark round spots upon it. The eye possesses wonderful brilliancy. It may be used as soon as the Green Drake goes out, for about three weeks (i.e. towards the middle or end of June).
- This pattern without the orange tinsel at the head has been used to imitate the green lacewing *Chrysopidae* (*Chrysopa flava*). The loop of orange tinsel is used specifically to imitate the golden gauze wing variety of lacewing (*Neuroptera*).
- Some patterns use a body of insect green wool or bright green silk (Pritt, 1885).
- The Green Sleeves was included in Lister's (1898) list of flies for the River Wharfe. Lister's pattern included the darkest feather from under the woodcock's wing. Head, magpie herl. Body, green silk. His remarks were: 'appears in June, well taken at times.' The pattern was tied to imitate a green bug (*Hemiptera*).
- According to Fogg (1988), the traditional Green Lacewing pattern can be regarded as a lighter-coloured version of the Green Woodcock.
- The use of bright green tinsel coated in clear varnish, the paler partridge feather and use of green with a loop of orange tinsel in the formation of the head, demonstrates JW's eye for detail in providing a pattern to specifically imitate the golden eyed gauze wing.

Mike Reed's comments: Standard tying; fine green tinsel looks good varnished.

Fog Black

A very small fly, resembling a flat winged needle in appearance, hatches out in the fog of newly mown meadows. A very good fly indeed and, in its season, the grayling has a fondness for this fly.

HOOK: 16

HACKLE: The white hackle from the silk bantam hen.

BODY: Very dark purple, almost black silk.

HEAD: Black silk.

Comments
• This pattern is different from T. E. Pritt's Little Black which used a dark glossy purple-black feather from the starling's neck for the hackle. The Little Black when dressed with a bullfinch wing (starling feather slips are now generally used) becomes T. E. Pritt's Fog Black. JW's pattern of the Fog Black differs in that it has a white hackle from the silk bantam hen and did not include the wings from starling slips. It is therefore questionable whether this fly is a true representation of the Fog Black.
• T. E. Pritt used his pattern of the Little Black on cold days in March and April, on cool summer days, and during late August and September.
• T. E. Pritt considered his pattern of the Fog Black to be his favourite top dropper for grayling.
• Fog is the name given in Upper Wharfedale to the lush grass which grows after haymaking. The small black member of the *Diptera* order lives on the lush grass and finds its way onto the water.
• Perhaps JW's pattern is an imitation of a light needle fly (stonefly) *Leuctra fusca* as noted in its use. This stonefly appears from February to April. The hackle may suggest the wings of the natural fly, it is worth noting that the wings are pale when the insect is newly emerged and then gradually darken as time passes (Fogg, 1988). Stoneflies do not hatch in the stream, the nymphs crawl onto the land before metamorphosing into adult flies.

Mike Reed's comments: Twist black and purple silk together and wax to make the body.

Hackled Greenwell

HOOK: **14**

HACKLE: **Small feather taken from under a young waterhen wing before first moult.**

BODY: **Yellow silk waxed with green-olive wax and ribbed with four turns of gold tinsel.**

THORAX: **Blue fox rabbit fur.**

RECIPE FOR WAX: **Add together 2oz of amber and ¼oz beeswax and two dessert spoonfuls of turpentine. Allow to boil for half an hour and then add a small quantity of yellow dye. When thoroughly mixed, pour out into a basin of cold water.**

The dressing for the Hackled Greenwell was published in the Fishing Gazette, 1943, but did not appear in JW's notebook of wet fly dressings.

Mike Reed's comments: Blue fox fur is substituted with rabbit grey under fur.

Chelker Greenwell

HOOK: 14

BODY: Flat Silver tinsel body coated with a transparent yellowish varnish.

THORAX: Olive-grey-green or olive dyed opossum fur used for lining shuttles *[JW's original patterns apparently used a dubbing clipped from a woollen carpet remnant].* Ribbing of fine gold wire.

HACKLE: Coch-y-bondhu hen hackle.

WINGS: Split wing of blackbird or starling primary feather which is tied upright to the body.

TAG: Tag of fluorescent red wool (Gantron) or Saville's DRF Fluorescent Wool shade 505 Fire Orange (Scarlet).

Comments

• JW also developed a pattern known as the Chelker Greenwell and this pattern is an extremely useful fly for reservoir fishing. The Chelker Greenwell has a split wing (of blackbird or starling primary feather) which is upright rather than low over the body, a flat silver tinsel body coated with a transparent yellowish varnish, a conspicuous olive-grey-green thorax (dubbing originally clipped from a woollen carpet remnant but subsequently of olive dyed opossum fur used for lining shuttles) ribbed with fine gold wire, a Coch-y-bondhu hen hackle, and a red tag originally of fluorescent red wool (Gantron) but a similar shade would appear to be Saville's DRF Fluorescent Wool shade 505 Fire Orange (Scarlet).

• The Chelker Greenwell, used as a top dropper in various sizes, has caught many brown, rainbow and sea trout from still waters and rivers throughout the UK. It is an interesting example of an innovative pattern, developed and tested about fifty years ago for use on Chelker Reservoir which lies between Addingham and Skipton. In past years there were big hatches of chironomids (including dark olives (*Baetis scambus*) and pond olives (*Cloeon dipterum*) in May and June, but such prolific hatches have decreased since a pipeline was installed for the almost continuous infusion of aerated River Wharfe and Barden Reservoir waters. However, it remains a very useful fly which has been used with great success by many anglers and apparently 'rediscovered' several times according to the angling press. It resembles Bob Church's June Fly (Church, 1987) and the tag of red fluorescent wool is a common feature in many modern reservoir flies.

Mike Reed's comments: Odd-looking fly, but a pretty standard tying.

Hackled Iron Blue Dun

Excellent in a running-off water after a spate throughout April, May, June and July. The second edition, which hatches in August, should be tied with a hackle from outside the wing of a merlin hawk.

HOOK: 16

HACKLE: Small feather from outside the blue tit wing.

BODY: Quill of the small feathers on the outside of a coot wing; flatten the quill in the jaws of a vice before stripping.

THORAX: Mole fur.

HEAD: Orange-brown artificial silk, one turn only.

This dressing was published in the Fishing Gazette, 1943, but did not appear in JW's notebook of wet fly dressings.

Comments

• Iron blue dun (*Baetis niger/B. muticus*).

• Hatches at the surface in open water during the day throughout the summer with peaks in May and September.

• The Hackled Iron Blue is included in F. M. Halfords book, *Floating Flies and How to Dress Them* (1886). Halford's pattern included; hackle of dark blue dun cock, body of quill split from a feather of old starling or coot wing, and whisk form dark blue dun cock's beard hackle.

Mike Reed's comments: The blue tit hackle looks grey to me, so use a waterhen hackle from the leading edge of the wing. The quill body is the centre quill feather flattened, I use finger nails.

Claret Landrail

Some dressers of this fly prefer the red cock pheasant tail herl for the body but the above dressing does very well in a big water in August and September. Apart from trout in rivers and reservoirs it is a very good sea trout fly, especially in Norway.

HOOK: 12

HACKLE: A reddish hackle from outside the wing of a Landrail.

BODY: Dubbing of claret artificial silk ribbed with orange tinsel.

HEAD: Peacock herl and orange silk.

Comments

• In John Swarbrick's manuscript *List of Flies for the River Wharfe* (1807), he includes a dressing for the Large Sun Fly. 'Large Sun Flie – take the feather ought of the inside of a Land Rale wing, oringe silk and peacock harl (No. 27).' JW's Claret Landrail may be an adaptation of Swarbrick's Large Sun Fly.

• T. E. Pritt's book *North Country Flies* (1886) included a dressing for the Thornfly Dun (No. 49) which is the same dressing as JW's Claret Landrail but without the dubbing of claret artificial silk ribbed with orange tinsel. Pritt noted this to be 'A very excellent fly in good bold brown water on warm days in summer, from June onwards'. Pritt commented that this fly is a variation of The Brown Owl, and equally useful. Dressed with a redder feather it is the same fly as that known as Blacker's Red.

• The pattern is possibly designed to imitate the Claret Dun (*Leptophlebia vespertina*); emergence during the day from early May to September.

Mike Reed's comments: Use the red/brown feather from the leading edge of a woodcock wing. The claret dub body can be made with mohair dubbed very thinly.

Grey Drake

This is a good wet imitation but I think the Grey Duster given in Courtney Williams book, or Baigent's Brown fished dry are quite as good. The natural has the habit of appearing with the Dark Watchet so one should have both wet patterns on the cast together. An alternative wet pattern is the Grey Partridge.

HOOK: 10, longshank.

WINGS: Hen pheasant primaries.

BODY: Olive fibro-silk ribbed with pale orange silk and yellow tinsel.

LEGS: Grey partridge dyed brownish olive.

TAIL: Three fibres from a partridge tail feather.

Comments

• Pattern tied to imitate a female spinner mayfly or spent gnat (*Ephemera danica*). While ovipositing the female spinner will often alight on the water for short periods, and at this stage she is referred to as the grey drake. Trout seem to prefer the spinner to the hatching dun and take them readily.

• The female spinner has transparent wings with a blue tint and brown veins. The abdomen is pale cream colour; the last three segments have brown streaks. The legs are dark olive/brown with the forelegs black/brown, and the three tails are dark brown.

• Emergence in May and June in the late afternoon and early evening in the vicinity of trees along the river bank.

Mike Reed's comments: The body is made from Uni-Glo floss, 600 denier phosphorescent white, take a bunch of fibres and tie them together, this can then be dipped into a simmering pan of yellow dye; this way you can control the dying process. Remove the fibres and wipe with kitchen paper to check the dying.

Skimming Midge

When the trout are midging, this is the fly to fish. When the midges are knotting and falling on the water or skating on the surface and dipping onto the water, they are eagerly looked for and the rises are vigorous. The novice may well be perturbed and get over exited and strike too hard and breakages will occur. The best way is to keep the first finger of the casting hand on the rod and keep cool. Don't let the rises get you muddled and don't curse the fish; blame yourself for letting the trout get you so het up. Fish upstream partially dry; that's a dry cast but not the fly, which should be fished just under the surface when they are seen better than through the surface film.

HOOK: **16 or 17**
HACKLE: **A black and**
white badger hen hackle.
BODY: **Black tying silk**
or black quill.
HEAD: **Black silk.**

Comments

• The trout often become selective when feeding on these and are difficult to tempt. These small midges and the small red and brown midges usually hatch in rivers during late evenings.

• Pattern to imitate a small black midge (*Polypedilum nubeculosus*). A very small species (3.5mm). The adult has a blackish body and legs with whitish wings. This and similar species are common and widespread, and hatches are often prolific during the late evening or early morning during the latter half of the summer.

Mike Reed's comments: Standard tying, super little pattern.

Hackled Early Olive

This is good in spring and autumn months
on most northern rivers and streams, and
can be dressed a little lighter as the season
advances with feathers from a coot wing or
pewit neck. It can be fished when the early
olive or large dark olive is on the water.

HOOK: 1 (or 12)

HACKLE: Feather from under coverts of a
young waterhen.

BODY: Peacock quill bleached in Parazone. After winding
give a coat of transparent pale yellow Cellire varnish.

THORAX: Mole fur.

HEAD: Yellow silk, well waxed.

Pattern also published in the Fishing Gazette, 1943.

Comments

• The early olive is a popular name for the large dark olive (*Baetis rhodani*). Most
imitations are known by the latter name.

• Prefers faster flowing water. The medium to large size adults appear from late February
to late April, and may reappear during a spell of mild autumn weather. Consequently it
is a useful grayling fly in addition to being an early-season trout fly.

• In early spring the duns often stay on the water for quite a long time, drying their
wings in a cold, damp atmosphere. Many northern rivers experience prolific hatches,
and even on the most unlikely days there may be a short rise period when trout take
the newly emerged duns.

Mike Reed's comments: Young birds have lighter coloured feathers than adult, worth
remembering when selecting one. The transparent yellow varnish is a mix of clear
cellire and yellow cellire varnish.

Dark Needle

One needs an array of needle flies to be successful when trout are needling,
that is when the fly fishing tests the angler's patience but don't worry; the
above dressings will prove their undoing. Another killing pattern is hackled
with the feather from under a swift's wing with a body of stripped peacock
quill. The sandpiper hackle with an orange/brown silk body is good for
grayling later in the season.

HOOK: 15

HACKLE: From a variety of colours e.g. fieldfare rump, a dark feather from outside the wing of the brown owl, a brown-olive sandpiper hackle, a dark bloa feather from outside the wing of a snipe, the under wing feather from a snipe.

BODY: A variety of colours e.g. dark clover, dark claret, copper, very dark purple, orange brown or ash coloured.

Comments

• Pattern used to imitate the needle fly (*Leuctra fusca/L. hippopus*), part of the stonefly group or hard-winged flies. Needle flies are slim and needle-like in appearance, it has hard shiny wings that appear to mould around the body. Both wings and body are dark brown. This fly should have a very slim tying-silk body which makes it an appropriate imitation of the needle-flies.

• The *Leuctra fusca* species occurs in all types of water with stony sub-strata. The peak flight period is from August to October. *Leuctra hippopus* is an early season species most common from February to April.

• T. E. Pritt's Dark Spanish Needle used a feather from the darkest part of a brown owl's wing. However, the Dark Spanish Needle is often dressed with a very dark brown hen feather (Fogg, 1988).

• Taff Price (1976) provided a popular pattern of brown silk thread, a body of thinly spun orange and brown seal's fur, brown cock pheasant hackle and a thin dark brown hen wing quill tied flat across the back.

Mike Reed's comments: Again use the outer covert feather from the edge of a woodcock wing.

Light Needle

A very good fly indeed when the trout are after the needle flies. Sometimes on with the Dark Needles. The needle fly bodies need careful watching as they appear in many colours. I've seen them even a clover shade, sometimes claret, then again copper and sometimes almost black: influenced I dare say by the weather or colour feeding from various plants or leaves on the trees.

HOOK: 15

HACKLE: Feather from under a sand grouse wing if obtainable. The light feather from under the snipe wing will kill but I would use the sand grouse hackle if possible.

BODY: Pale orange shading to apricot.

HEAD: Orange silk

Comments

• There are more than one species of stonefly known as the needle fly (*Leuctra fusciventris*). All are very similar in appearance, being small and, as their name suggests, thin and needle-like. They are the smallest of the species, making their first appearance around May time and continue to emerge right throughout the season. T. E. Pritt gave many patterns of stoneflies and recognised the darker and lighter coloured versions.

• Michael Theakston (1853) tied the Light Spanish Needle with a light bloa feather from underneath a snipe's wing. T. E. Pritt (1885) tied the Light Spanish Needle with either a hackle feather from the inside of a snipe's wing or from the breast of a young starling; the body was tied with crimson silk with a peacock herl head.

• Pritt (1885) suggested that this fly was more suitable for warm days. The shades of the natural flies vary considerably.

• It is interesting to note Taff Price's comment about the stonefly family, 'If the upwing flies of the chalk stream are classed as jewels, then the stoneflies to the angler of the rough stream must at least be semi-precious stones, for without them the rivers would be that much poorer' (Price, 1976).

Mike Reed's comments: Standard tying. You sometimes see sand grouse sold as a snipe alternative.

Green Owl

A good fly on a cold evening or a wet day. The wings of the natural are almost black or a very dark dun shade and lie in the sedge position. I've known this fly last some five or six weeks and will kill when least expected. When sedges are on, it is as well to examine the insects for you may find the Green Owl amongst them.

HOOK: 14

HACKLE: The dark feather from the outside of a brown owl wing.

BODY: Pea green tinsel.

HEAD: A turn of peacock herl and a loop of pea green tinsel.

Comments

• There is very little information about this particular fly dressing in the angling literature. It would appear that JW tied this fly to resemble hatching sedges or possibly sedge pupae. This pattern is therefore similar to the Green Woodcock in this respect. Possibly tied to imitate the sand-fly (*Rhyacophila dorsalis*), the marbled sedge (*Hydropsyche contubernalis*) or the grannom (*Brachycentrus subnubilus*). These three sedges may possess a green or greenish brown body. In particular, the female grannom egg sac imparts a green tinge to the body. Whatever the theory of its imitation, it is quite true that at times trout are simply and inexplicibly on to a certain colour and will look at nothing else. Perhaps this might have something to do with the state of the water, the light or the weather.

• Although this fly was once dressed with a feather from the brown owl, it now must be tied with a rather coarse fibred red/brown hen hackle or possibly a french partridge marginal covert feather dyed to the appropriate shade.

Mike Reed's comments: Again, use the brown woodcock wing hackle.

Copper Partridge

This, of course, is the snuff brown may fly or the hackled pattern of the freckled dun and great sport can be had when this fly is on the water, usually at about the same time as the sand fly. Some name this fly the brown watchet. There are some reservoirs in Yorkshire where this fly often appears and may be made a little larger for that purpose.

HOOK: 13 or 14

HACKLE: Dark brown partridge, well dappled.

BODY: Copper silk, about the shade of a new penny.

HEAD: Copper silk.

Pattern also published in the Fishing Gazette, 1943.

Comments

• Very old pattern dating back to Williamson (1740) and Bowlker (1747). Some old dressings used dark orange silk dubbed with bear's down (Fogg, 1988).

• Pattern possibly tied to imitate the iron blue dun (*Baetis muticus*). However, probably better imitation of a Stonefly (*Amphinemoura, taeniopterix nebulosa, nemoura sps. Leuctra sps*).

• Included in list of artificial flies used by Sylvester Lister Snr., Barden Tower, near

Bolton Abbey (1898). Lister's pattern included the feather from the back of a merlin hawk. Head, orange silk. Body, orange and purple twisted with a little mole's fur. Lister remarks: a very small fly but a favourite on cold blustery days.

• The Copper Partridge is very similar to John Turton's Dark Moor Game (Moorgame and Orange) which used a very dark freckled feather from the 'knuckle' of a dark cock red grouse wing and Michael Theakston's Freckled Dun which used a grouse feather for the hackle.

Mike Reed's comments: Use Uni Micro Tinsel for a nice body with extra flash; I suspect this would be a good fly in peat stained water.

Orange Partridge

This fly can be safely used in a coloured water all through the season. Some of the body dressings may be new to most tiers but they can be assured that they are better for attraction, especially the red tinsel eyes.

HOOK: 14

HACKLE: A well dappled feather, fairly dark, from the partridge back.

BODY: A rich orange silk ribbed with orange tinsel, or can use orange tinsel coated with transparent varnish or, for a transparent body, apply a layer of orange cellulose varnish over silver tinsel.

THORAX: Red bronze peacock herl.

Comments

• As a nymph-suggesting trout fly for fast streams and even for lake fishing when there is a bit of a wave there are few soft hackled patterns to equal this one. It is regarded as a fail-me-never by anglers up and down the county. Few anglers who fish the rivers of Yorkshire would care to be without it (Stewart, 1964). According to Oldfield (1986), 'Where the rivers flow swift over rocky beds, I will back this ancient fly against modern creations.'

• The several extant examples of this fly tied by JW have all been dressed with a hackle feather giving a barb length one and half times the overall hook length and are thus longer than the hackles used for his other partridge flies which have the more typical hackle length only slightly longer than the hook length.

• According to Roger Fogg (1988) the Orange Partridge probably began life as an imitation of the February red stonefly (*Taeniopteryx nebulosa*) for specific use on northern rivers (Pilling, 1794; Swarbrick, 1807). Originally intended as an early season pattern, its use had already become far more extensive by 1885, when T. E. Pritt declared that 'it would kill from April to September, on warm days. So effective a fly is it, that it will do equally well on stillwaters and will frequently catch fish when conventional patterns fail.' Pritt's recommended cast for northern river fishing from the middle of April to the end of June was: tail fly March Brown, first dropper Snipe Bloa, second dropper Iron Blue Dun and third dropper Orange Partridge.

• The February Red is an early season fly and is seen usually between February and April. *Brachyptera risi* is more common and widespread than *T. nebulosa* and its season is longer, extending from March to July, and in some areas may also be referred to as the February red. It is similar in size to *T. nebulosa*, but often found in small stony streams as well as slower-paced rivers.

• A favourite fly of W. Brumfitt (1875) of Otley. Also included in Sylvester Lister's (1898) *List of Flies for the Wharfe*. Lister also referred to the Orange Partridge as the Brown Watchett. His pattern included the brownish speckled feather from the back of a partridge. Head: magpie herl. Body: orange silk, well waxed. He remarked that the Orange Partridge was 'a good fly all season through'. Lister said that the Orange Partridge pattern not only imitated the stonefly but also the blue-winged olive nymph (*Ephemerella ignita*).

• T. E. Pritt said that the Orange Partridge was the same pattern as the Turkey Brown of Ronalds, and the Spiral Drake of Theakston.

• The Orange Partridge has similarities to some *Ephemeropteran* species such as March brown (*Rithrogena germanica*), and depending on how it is fished it may pass for a spinner.

• Roger Fogg (1988) also noted that a rib of narrow gold or silver tinsel adds extra attraction especially for grayling. The tinsel is also useful when the fly is to be fished in tumbling currents; the extra sparkle makes it more easily noticed.

Mike Reed's comments: Varnished fluo. Use orange floss and silk to make a segmented body.

Claret Partridge

A good imitation of the August Brown and should be fished at point during a hatch of the natural. It is a very good killer and should be used in preference to the winged pattern on Yorkshire rivers.

HOOK: 12

HACKLE: A very dark, well mottled partridge hackle.

BODY: Claret dubbing ribbed with yellow silk.

HEAD: peacock herl.

Comments

• Possibly an imitation of the August dun (*Ecdyrus longicanda),* turkey brown dun /spinner (*Paraleptophlebia submarginata*), purple dun (*Paraleptophlebia cincta*) or claret dun (*Leptophlebia vespertina*).

• According to Alfred Ronalds (1836) the August dun comes from a water nympha, lives two or three days, then changes to a red spinner. It is in season from the beginning of August to the middle of September.

• Francis Walbran also claimed the August Brown to be a good grayling fly.

• W. H. Lawrie described the Partridge and Claret to be a killing spring fly on the Tweed and other Scottish Border rivers.

• Roger Fogg (1988) and Courtney Williams (1973) included a pattern called the Welsh Partridge. This had claret coloured silk, with body of roughly dubbed purple seal's fur ribbed with fine oval gold tinsel, hackle of brown partridge feather and dark crimson hen, tail of pheasant tippets. Fogg said that this fly was extremely good on the top dropper for reservoir rainbow fishing.

Mike Reed's comments: Use a mohair dub for the body, Jim Wynn may well have had some.

Rough Bodied Poult

A rare killer on a summer evening. This is one of Edmonds & Lee's dressings and must not be confused with the Rusty Poult.

HOOK: 14

HACKLE: Hackled with a light blue feather from the under coverts of a young grouse wing (the lighter side of the feather towards the head of the fly).

BODY: Straw coloured silk dubbed with fawn opossum fur.

HEAD: Straw coloured silk.

Comments

• Edmonds and Lee (1916) pattern tied to imitate one of the *Ephemeridae* which appear on the Wharfe in July, August and September. Pattern possibly taken as a small dark olive (*Baetis scambus*), large dark olive (*Baetis rhodani*) and olive dun (*Rithrogena semicolorata*).

• Alternative for opossum fur – medium olive seal fur.

Mike Reed's comments: The opossum can be substituted with fawn rabbit. Always buy whole skins – that way you get a range of colours.

Tangerine Partridge

Excellent in coloured water throughout the
spring and summer months. May be fished as
the first dropper to a Red Partridge at point.

HOOK: 14

BODY: Tangerine cellulose acetate art silk ribbed
with four turns of orange tinsel.

THORAX: Red bronze peacock herl over which wind
a very dark brown partridge hackle.

HEAD: One turn of red tinsel

*Dressing published in the Fishing Gazette, 1943, but did not appear in JW's notebook
of wet fly dressings.*

Comments

• This is probably one of JW's creations. Similar to the Copper King which had brown
tying thread, hackle of brown speckled partridge back feather with a body of copper
foil or tinsel. The Copper King was generally regarded as a grayling fly; it may be
leaded so that it will fish deep in pools where winter grayling hug the bottom in shoals.
However, this pattern was also employed for trout fishing on hot summer days and
thought to do well in amber-coloured/peat stained Pennine reservoirs.

• This pattern is also similar to Sylvester Lister's (1895) Light Partridge. This pattern
included a light freckled feather from the partridge back. Head: gold tinsel. Body: straw
coloured gold tinsel. This pattern was tied to imitate a primrose spinner (*Heptagenia
sulphurea*).

• It should also be noted that the Tangerine Partridge is also not dissimilar to the
March Brown Spider which used a light orange tying thread, a well speckled partridge
back feather and a body comprised of a mixture of various shades of hare's ear fur
dubbed on pale orange silk and ribbed with yellow silk. The March Brown Spider was
used on the Derbyshire rivers at least during the eighteenth-century.

Mike Reed's comments: Varnished fluo. Orange floss for the rib, Uni Micro Tinsel for
the head.

Purple Partridge

This is rather an unknown fly to many Yorkshire tiers. It was a favourite of
J. W. Binns, one time landlord of the Red Lion Hotel at Burnsall, and was
often used by J. Hudson, keeper of the Bolton Abbey waters some years ago.
The natural is generally on the water towards the end of May and early June.

HOOK: 14

HACKLE: A very dark partridge hackle, one that is almost black with a light mottle towards or half way up towards the tip.

BODY: Dark purple silk or purple tinsel with a coat of varnish.

HEAD: Purple silk and a turn of peacock herl.

Comments

• The several extant examples of this fly tied by JW have all been dressed with a hackle length one and a half times the overall hook length, and are thus longer than the hackles used for his other partridge flies which have the more typical hackle barb length only slightly longer than the hook length.

• This appears to be very similar to the very old partridge-hackled fly known as the Orl Fly. It is now rarely used yet once enjoyed considerable popularity. This is an imitation of the alder ('Orl' being a local name for this fly) it began to lose popularity after the standard winged pattern was introduced. The winged dressing is often credited to Charles Kingsley, although it should be attributed to Alfred Ronalds. The Orl Fly is included in John Turton's book, *The Angler's Manual* (1836). Turton's pattern used a dark red or wine coloured tying thread. Hackle, a dark brown speckled partridge back feather. Body, bronze peacock herl over dark red tying silk. A tag of tying silk may be left at the end of the body.

• According to Fogg (1988), 'while the Orl Fly will catch its quota of river trout, it is a good 'sedgey' stillwater fly and probably suggests other succulent items of food, including beetles and various larvae. I suppose that it might be regarded as a 'fancy' fly, yet it does suggest a variety of food forms.'

Mike Reed's comments: Standard tying.

Red Partridge

The body may be dressed with dark red silk and ribbed with orange tinsel but I prefer the red tinsel for brightness. The fly is as useful as the Orange Partridge and should never be omitted from the cast throughout the trout season. You must be sure to put both Orange and Red Partridge flies on the cast after a spate when the water is still coloured and fining down. You will be nearly certain to have excellent results from May to the end of the season.

HOOK: 14

HACKLE: Greyish brown partridge wound palmerwise over the thorax. Clip off spare fibres above and below the thorax, leaving the remaining fibres on each side.

BODY: Red tinsel ribbed with 4 or 5 turns of red tinsel.

THORAX: Peacock herl.

HEAD: Peacock herl with a loop of red tinsel for eyes.

Pattern also published in the Fishing Gazette, 1943.

Comments

• This pattern together with the Crimson Partridge (J. Blades, 1887) was probably tied to imitate the February red stonefly (*Taeniopteryx nebulosa*).

• Common in the North of England, however, according to Goddard (1976) it is the only stonefly which dislikes a stony environment, being more partial to slow-flowing rivers with much vegetation.

• The February red is an early season fly and is seen usually between February and April. *Brachyptera risi* is more common and widespread than *T. nebulosa* and its season is longer, extending from March to July and in some areas may also be referred to as the February red. It is similar in size to *T. nebulosa*, but often found in small stony streams as well as slower-paced rivers.

• It is medium to small, and has red-brown wings, marked with two dark bands, the last three body segments being a reddish brown colour.

• According to Roger Fogg (1988) this pattern does well whenever the river is discoloured. The fly also fishes well in peaty little lochs and may be used on a traditional loch-style cast when boat fishing.

Mike Reed's comments: Fiddly to tie, but a nice looking pattern. Use Uni Micro Tinsel for body and eyes.

Yellow Partridge

A very good imitation of a hatching olive nymph, especially good when trout are underwater feeding just before a spate comes along when the becks have coloured the sides of the river. One of my own creations for that purpose.

HOOK: 14

HACKLE: A brownish partridge hackle, well defined. Strip hackle on one side before tying in and wind between the ribs of the herl forming the thorax, then use a little pressure to force back the herl over the hackle stem.

Clip fibres from above and below the thorax leaving a few on either side.

BODY: Abdomen, two thirds of silver tinsel coated with a transparent yellow varnish, or yellow cellulose acetate thread ribbed with yellow tinsel.

THORAX: A single fibre of cock pheasant tail.

TAIL: Two short strands from a cock pheasant tail.

Pattern also published in the Fishing Gazette, 1943.

Comments

• Pattern thought to resemble medium olive nymph (*Baetis vernus*) or olive upright nymph (*Rhithrogena semicolorata*).

• Very old wet fly pattern, included in Swarbrick's lists (1807). Also included in the list of artificial flies used by Lister (1898). Lister's pattern used a fine speckled feather from the back of partridge; head, yellow; sometimes ribbed with gold wire. He remarked that the Yellow Partridge was taken as 'large *Ephemera* in early May. Capital throughout season. Well taken when Dark Watchet is on.'

• According to Roberts (1995) a good early season fly, probably giving the best results in the evening from April to June.

• Richard Walker achieved considerable success with short-bodied Orange and Yellow Partridges dressed on large hooks which possessed reasonably long shanks.

Mike Reed's comments: Standard materials but a complex little fly. Tie the tail and body materials in first, then make a half hitch. Make six half-flies before applying the varnish. Let these dry before you finish tying the rest of the fly.

Green Poult

This fly appears about the longest day of the year, June 21st, and continues at intervals until October. The natural is an upright winged fly of small dimensions, about the size of an iron blue dun. It is a good killer late in the evenings in summer, yet I've seen it on the water and being used to kill fish in August 12th during the mid-day rise. Was first shown to me by J. Hudson of Bolton Abbey and was one of his specials. It is a fly not generally known by the 'Yorkshire Tiers'. It may be fished dry with an appropriate cock hackle, a medium blue Andalusian.

HOOK: 16

HACKLE: From under a young grouse wing.

BODY: Of green silk, about the shade of the underside of a new holly leaf, ribbed with yellow tinsel.

HEAD: Green silk as for body.

Comments

• Pattern probably used to imitate a July dun or August dun (*Ephemeridae*) or pale watery olives.

• The feather is the small, mottled, red-brown, marginal covert feather from the wing of a red grouse.

• A thorax of peacock herl or hare's ear may be added.

• This pattern is also known as the Green Grouse. For rivers the Green Poult should be tied on small hook sizes. However, the pattern can be tied on larger hook sizes for stillwater fishing.

• Fogg (1988) suggests the pattern is also taken as sedge pupae and the Green Grouse is capable of matching the success of most lake nymphs on still waters. During the day time on stillwaters they are best fished deep down, for which purpose they may be weighted with lead foil, while in the evening they may be fished close to the surface. When sedges are appearing and skittering along the water, which usually occurs as the light fades, you may even employ a quick retrieve with short pauses in between. In this way, the flies will not only fish close to the surface but will also provide enough surface disturbance to attract the attention and stimulate the trout's feeding instinct.

Mike Reed's comments: In the absence of young grouse, use a light coloured feather from an adult grouse.

Rusty Poult or Aldam's Indian Yellow

This is a good killer. Some may have difficulty in getting the right shade of dubbing. Many use fur from the young hare or leveret, others use the rusty fur from a red squirrel. However, the correct shade can only be derived by dyeing which gives a shade of its own. I don't know of any undyed fur that would make the correct body for this fly. Whilst being a good fly for trout, I've known it take its share of grayling in the season for that fish.

HOOK: 14

HACKLE: Very young grouse poult underwing.

BODY: Dubbing of fur from the nape of a rabbit's neck dyed a rusty shade in dye of equal parts tangerine and yellow dyes. It must be ribbed with Indian Yellow silk.

HEAD: Indian Yellow silk

Comments

• The Rusty Poult isn't actually a North Country fly but is a very good dry fly and a fine imitation of the blue winged olive (*Ephemerella ignite*). Emergence end of May and through summer.

• Halford popularised the pattern as a floating fly in 1886 and credited it to W. H. Aldam who published his book some ten years before Halford's *Floating Flies and How to Dress Them*. However, as the fly is mentioned in the fifth edition of Alfred Ronalds' *Fly-Fisher's Entomology*, it is probably of much earlier origin and may well have begun life as a wet fly. This is interesting as JW included this fly in his list of wet flies. Halford's dressing included as follows. Tying thread: lemon or primrose yellow. Hackle: pale, buff coloured Cochin silk. Body: floss silk about the colour of 'natural Russia leather', ribbed with bright-lemon coloured tying silk. Wings: inside grouse wing from a young bird.

• R. S. Austin in his *Manuscript Book of Dry-fly Fishing on Exe and other North Devon Streams* (1890) included a pattern called the Rusty Dun. This pattern included as follows. Body: rust coloured fur, half pink opossum, half hare's poll. Tying silk: cream. Hackle: light blue cock. Whisks: light blue cock. Wings: darkish starling.

Mike Reed's comments: Dying the rabbit was the only tricky bit, use several bits of fur so you can leave some in for longer, then you can select the best bit.

Yellow Poult

The body may be made with waxed yellow silk over which rib yellow tinsel and then give the whole a coating of transparent yellow acetate varnish. A fly which is accepted as a long standing pattern on Yorkshire rivers and a dressing which probably dates back to the early 1800s. I can trace it back to 1847. The acetate varnished body is an improvement on the old fashioned silk body. I've known it kill better when the hackle is pulled up for a single wing.

HOOK: 14

HACKLE: Feather taken from under the young grouse wing, taken before the first moult.

BODY: Yellow artificial silk that darkens to a yellow green when wet, and ribbed with yellow tinsel.

HEAD: Yellow silk.

Comments

• Pattern thought to imitate the pale wateries (*Baetis fuscatus*) or spurwings (*Centroptilum luteolum, C. pennulatum*). Present from May to October, main hatches in May.

• This pattern is very similar to the Yellow Spider Fly included within John Turton's book *The Angler's Manual* (1836). This is a significant piece of work because many of the standard North Country flies, often erroneously accredited to Pritt, appear for the first time in print within its pages.

- Turton recommended the Yellow Spider Fly to be used in June when the river was clear and low. It is a similar fly to the Yellow Grouse.
- Turton's pattern included, hook, size 16 or 14. Tying thread, light yellow silk. Hackle, light brown mottled moorgame's feather (Fogg (1988) suggests feather taken from the marginal coverts of a female red grouse). Body, light yellow silk with light dubbing of yellow marten's fur taken from the throat of the animal.

Mike Reed's comments: Standard tying.

Dark Sedge

The counterpart is the Light Sedge, same body but hackle with a landrail feather, one that is mottled at the tip. These flies are useful in the evenings, more so when there happens along a spate during the summer. If one wishes to fish dry then a good ginger cock hackle will suffice for a floater.

HOOK: 14

HACKLE: From outside the brown owl wing to give a ginger red hackle.

BODY: Yellow silk dubbed with reddish hare's fur and ribbed with yellow tinsel.

HEAD: Yellow silk and a turn of cock pheasant tail herl.

Comments

- Pattern probably tied to resemble the medium sedge (*Goera pilosa*). It is medium-sized with broad wings, about 11mm long, that are greyish/yellow to darker yellow. It is one of the hairier species.
- This species of sedge is very widely distributed and abundant, and is most common during the early summer in May and June. This is a very useful sedge pattern to the trout fisherman, as it is also one of the day-flying species.
- Although this fly was once dressed with a feather from the brown owl it now must be tied with a rather coarse fibred red/brown hen hackle or possibly a french partridge marginal covert feather dyed to the appropriate shade.
- Francis Francis' book entitled, *A Book on Angling* (1867) includes a pattern for the sedge fly which was tied to resemble the light sedge. This included as follows. Wings (full): starling under, landrail upper. Body: light buff crewel. Hackle (tail to head): pale red. Ribbing: fine gold wire run over the hackle the reverse way.
- The Dark Sedge and Light Sedge are included in Edmonds and Lee, *Brook and River Trouting* (1916). The Dark Sedge pattern included as follows. Wings: hackled with a reddish brown feather from the lesser coverts of a tawny or brown owl's wing. Body: yellow silk dubbed with brownish fawn seal's fur. Head: brownish green herl from the

tail of a cock pheasant. The Light Sedge pattern included as follows. Wings: hackled with a light-barred reddish feather from the lesser coverts of a landrail's wing. Body: yellow silk, dubbed with reddish fur from the thigh of a red squirrel. Head: a reddish herl from the tail of a cock pheasant.

Mike Reed's comments: Brown/red woodcock hackle from the outer covert wing feathers. The red hare can be found on that rabbit skin you've got.

Yellow Snipe

A hackled pattern of light olive dun. A feather from a fieldfare back may be used but the fly is then known as the Fieldfare Bloa. Some tiers add a touch of light dubbing which is not necessary in the fly. It is a first rate killer when the light olive duns are around and should not be neglected as a good spring pattern.

HOOK: 14

HACKLE: Feather from under the jacksnipe wing, a light dun hackle.

BODY: Yellow silk.

HEAD: Yellow silk.

This is the Light Snipe or Snipe Bloa of Edmonds & Lee.

Comments

• The Yellow Snipe is a pattern that probably represents a range of flies. The pattern may represent various yellow naturals such as yellow may duns (*Heptagenia sulphurea*), yellow evening duns (*Ephemerella notata*) and yellow sallies (*Isoperla grammatica*). It is also especially effective as imitations of various pale watery olives (*Baetis fuscatus*) and spurwings (*Centroptilum luteolum*). As pale wateries vary in shade, and individual species darken in colour as the season progresses, this may easily account for the lighter and darker artificial versions of this group of flies. The Yellow Snipe can do quite well to imitate the nymph of the blue winged olive. The Yellow Snipe can also be used as an early season or summer nymph pattern when fished slowly on still waters.

• An excellent old wet-fly pattern. The fly may be tied with a single layer of primrose floss over the tying silk under body. Theakston (1853) added a thorax of brown wool. A peacock herl thorax can also be used. The snipe feather is a lighter coloured marginal covert feather with a pale blotch at the tips and a distinct brown buff colour over all.

• A variation of this fly is tied with the feather from the marginal coverts of a golden plover wing; this is a mousey coloured hackle with deep yellow blotches around the edges. The yellow markings on the hackle harmonise with the body colour of the fly.

• The Snipe Bloa is a paler version of the Yellow Snipe and has straw-coloured silk and uses a pale bloa feather from the under coverts of a snipe wing. The feather must possess a general colouring of pale blue-grey. A similar fly is the Light Watchet which is hackled with a pale starling feather and is also given a straw-coloured silk body.

• Snipe hackled flies when wet look singularly unimpressive and austere but that is the very reason for their success; they are much closer to the delicacy of natural insects than most over-dressed and gaudy creations. Correctly-dressed, soft-hackled patterns will attract trout from rivers, streams and lakes; and sparsely dressed versions or ones where the hackle has been worn away to a ragged whisp may do even better.

Mike Reed's comments: The jack snipe hackle can be substituted with a normal snipe one.

Throstle Wing

A good late season fly and, if mild, can be used to the end of November for grayling.

HOOK: 14

HACKLE: The dark cinnamon feather from a landrail or from outside the throstle (thrush) wing as the name suggests.

BODY: Lead coloured silk dubbed with a mixture of reddish and dun coloured fur from a red squirrel.

HEAD: Peacock herl.

Comments

• This may be a version of Jackson's (1854) dressing of the alder fly (*Sialis lutaria*) which used a thrush feather. The alder is widely distributed throughout the country, the adult alder makes its appearance in late April, May and June and although very much a water-side insect, is not a water-bred one.

• Conceivably this pattern might be mistaken during the summer for many of the medium sized dark sedges, especially at dusk. As a grayling fly this pattern is probably taken as an olive upright (*Rithrogena semicolorata*) or the autumn dun (*Ecdyonurus dispar*). It would appear that JW's pattern was a late season fly and was therefore a pattern tied to resemble the olive upright or autumn dun.

• Some anglers say that during the mayfly season when the Green or Spent Drake fails to interest trout the Alder should be used.

• This pattern is possibly a hackled version of the Alder fly given by J. Jackson in his book *The Practical Fly-Fisher* (1854). It would appear that feathers from the thrush were used by the fly tyers Chetham from Lancashire (1681), Turton from Derbyshire (1836) and Swarbrick from Yorkshire (1807). Jackson's pattern for the Alder was as follows. Silk: lead coloured. Body: blue and brown squirrel's fur dubbed on the silk.

Wings: landrail or throstle (thrush). Hackle: a dark grizzled hen hackle.
• Sylvester Lister's (1898) pattern of the Alder for use on the River Wharfe was a winged version. Lister's dressing included: feather from the outside of a brown owl's wing; head – peacock herl; body – orange with brown peacock herl ribbed with fine gold wire. Lister recommended this fly from the mid-May to the end of the season.
• Skues pattern of the hackled Alder and the hackled version of the Herefordshire Alder were fished as dry flies. However, it should be noted that Canon C. F. Eagles dressing of the hackled Herefordshire Alder was fished wet; this pattern included a body of pheasant tail fibres over purple floss, with the floss showing as alternate rings. The hackle was of a brown dun coloured Andalusian cock feather.

Mike Reed's comments: Dye a starling body hackle cinnamon or use a lighter brown feather from the woodcock wing for this one. Rabbit is used instead of red squirrel.

Green Quail

Appears about the second week in May and is sometimes responsible for the first evening rises when the fish are generally on in profusion. A very good killing pattern.

HOOK: **14**
HACKLE: **Feather from the underside of the Egyptian Quail wing; if not available, then from under the young starling wing.**
BODY: **Dubbing of dark green art silk ribbed with yellow silk.**
HEAD: **Yellow silk.**

Comments
• Pattern tied to resemble pale coloured insects, including the pale wateries and various spinners (*Baetis fuscatus*).
• The palest starling feather from the under coverts should be used.
• This fly is similar to the Starling Bloa, Snipe and Yellow or Snipe Bloa.
• The Starling Bloa pattern included as follows. Hook: 18, 16 or 14. Tying thread: primrose or straw-coloured. Hackle: palest starling feather from the under coverts. Body: as tying silk, although a white tying silk body is sometimes used. The fly is much improved with a small thorax of the palest hare's ear fur dubbed behind the hackle. Head, an optional peacock herl head may be included.
• The Starling Bloa is also quite similar to one of the most popular soft hackled fly patterns of the nineteenth and early twentieth century, the Dotterel Dun.

Mike Reed's comments: As described, the art silk can be bought in hanks from craft/ haberdashery shops, a good place to shop for these materials.

Purple Water Rail

One of my own dressings akin to the Purple Snipe and made as a copy of that fly which turned out to be just as attractive or even better than the ordinary dressing. It must be noted that the hackle must be well selected to copy the wing of the natural. Great sport may be had if one uses two or even three copies of this fly when the trout are taking the natural.

HOOK: 14.

HACKLE: Taken from the neck or breast of the water rail; a feather which is of a particular blue shade and tipped with a fawnish shade at the extreme tip. Two turns only.

BODY: Purple tinsel coated with a transparent acetate varnish.

HEAD: Purple tinsel and a turn of peacock or magpie herl.

Pattern also published in the Fishing Gazette, 1943.

Comments

• JW's own dressing of a pattern similar to the Snipe and Purple. The Snipe and Purple is a dressing used to imitate the iron blue dun (*Baetis muticus*) and should do well when these naturals are in evidence on cool summer days. Appears from April onwards. This pattern will also imitate any of the darker *Ephemeropterans* including the purple dun (*Paraleptophlebia cinta*) on rivers and the sepia dun (*Leptophlebia marginata*) and claret dun (*Leptophlebia vespertina*) on stillwaters. This pattern may also be used on summer evenings when small black flies populate the river.

• Unfortunately, the common water-rail (*Rallus aquaticus*) of Europe is now extinct. Possibly use the snipe bluish back feathers, starling bluish breast and back feathers or guinea fowl blue neck feathers as a replacement.

• Can be fished as a point fly or can be used on the top dropper. Useful pattern for picking up stillwater trout feeding on midge pupae just under the surface film.

• A good general fly.

Mike Reed's comments: Look on that starling skin for the hackle; the body is varnished silk.

Purple Snipe or Dark Bloa

An alternative dressing has a body of purple tinsel, or silver tinsel coated with purple transparent acetate varnish, the latter gives an excellent transparent bodied wet fly. The winged pattern is made using starling primary quill feathers with black legs and a few strands of red, added for attraction, which do not exist in the natural fly. However, this fly is not the Broughton Point fly, the body of which is blue ultramarine.

HOOK: 14

HACKLE: Feather taken from under snipe wing in preference to the outside wing as used by most Yorkshire tiers.

BODY: Ruddy purple silk or mulberry shade of artificial silk dubbed onto purple silk.

Comments

• This fly is also known as the Snipe and Purple, Dark Snipe or Dark Bloa and Purple. The pattern is thought to imitate the iron blue dun (*Baetis muticus*) and it certainly does well on those cool summer days when these naturals are in evidence but it may be used as an imitation of any of the darker ephemeropterans. This would include such river flies as the purple dun (*Paraleptophlebia cinta*) and such lake flies as the sepia dun (*Leptophlebia marginata*) and claret dun (*Leptophlebia vespertina*). The pattern can be successful as an early season pattern and does well on summer evenings when small black flies populate the river. It is also a useful fly for grayling from September to November. In short, it will do well throughout the season.

• Probably one of the top five on most North Country angler's list of wet flies to use on northern rivers. This fly can be fished on the point but may also be fished on the top dropper.

• This pattern is very old and was included in M. Theakston's *British Angling Flies* (1853). He had a Dark Bloa pattern for March and a Dark Bloa pattern for August. The Dark Bloa (March pattern) included as follows. Body: red/brown silk. Wings: a dark feather from the inside of a waterhen's wing. Hackle: black cock or hen hackle. Tail: black cock hackle fibres. The pattern for the Dark Bloa (August pattern) was the same as the March pattern apart from the wings which could be tied with either the inside of a swift or a waterhen's wing and the hackle was of a dark brown hen hackle feather and a tail of a few fibres of a dark brown hen hackle.

• In T. E. Pritt's book *Yorkshire Trout Flies* (1885), he included a pattern for the Dark Bloa, but he also called this fly the Broughton's Point. However, JW said the Dark Bloa or Purple Snipe was not the Broughton's Point.

• Roger Fogg (1988) said that the Dark Bloa was a hackled version of the Broughton's Point, and a close relative of the Watchet. He said that the Dark Bloa was frequently given a jackdaw hackle rather than the more conventional black hen feather. Fogg considered the jackdaw hackle to make a better fly and presents a good imitation of the claret dun. He gave a pattern of the Dark Bloa as follows. Tying thread: dark claret or wine coloured silk. Hackle: a dark charcoal jackdaw throat feather. Body: claret floss silk. With the addition of wings from the dark starling primary quill, this becomes the Broughton's Point, a favoured fly in the Lake District.

• Some believe to dress the fly correctly you must be a real miser with your materials; the body must be short and slender while a single turn of hackle is sufficient. Although the fly may be dressed with a floss silk body, two layers of plain tying silk are quite sufficient. A typical dressing is as follows. Tying thread: unwaxed purple silk (Pearsall's Gossamer shade 8). Hackle: a dark marginal covert feather from the snipe, or jack snipe for preference, choose a spoon-shaped feather. Body: purple tying silk or floss silk. A neat little thorax of green peacock herl close up against the hackle is considered by some anglers to make a much improved fly.

• Watchets, Dark Watchets, Dark Bloas, Broughton's Point and the like are obviously closely related flies and imitations of dark ephemerals such as the iron blue and claret duns. It is generally true that seemingly different flies turn out to be merely regional variations on a much older basic dressing. At the same time, fly-fishermen in different areas may work independently in copying directly from nature and still coincidentally produce the same dressing. This is why it is so difficult for the angling historians to say who deserves the credit for certain patterns.

• The Snipe and Purple can be used for taking stillwater trout feeding on midge pupae. A small Snipe and Purple fished just under the surface film has proved successful on many visits to Pennine reservoirs and the River Wharfe.

• The expert grayling fisher, Reg Righyni, placed this fly as his favourite top dropper on a three-fly leader. He also incorporated a fine copper rib on some of his patterns. The soft snipe hackle can be worked in the current when the fly is fished upstream and this would seam to be a major factor in the pattern's representation of the nymph or duns struggling to emerge.

Mike Reed's comments: Dubbed silk on silk, fray the silk with your finger nails to make this; only Pearsalls Gossamer shade will do.

A Yorkshire Tie of Tups

This fly, a creation of mine for the surroundings during a hot summer evening when the sun having settled below the hills, leaves that pinky glow behind. It is for fish that become very active after a day of laziness when they are seeking out the pale duns that create the rise. This fly will settle all arguments of what they will rise to.

HOOK: **16 or 15**

HACKLE: **White hen is tipped with brassy sheen of red-orange or a feather from under a very young starling's wing taken not later than three weeks out of the nest, or a feather from under the Egyptian quail wing.**

BODY: **Two thirds (abdomen) of silver tinsel coated with transparent yellow varnish, the third portion of flesh pink tinsel coated with natural shade nail varnish.**

HEAD: **Yellow silk.**

Pattern also published in the Fishing Gazette, 1943.

Comments

• This Tups variant is a pale bodied dressing used to imitate the pale watery dun (*Baetis fuscatus*) or a small spurwing spinner – little sky-blue (*Centroptilum luteolum*). Use on summer evenings. The dressing may be varied to suggest a dun, or a nymph or a spinner. The original pattern by Austin was tied to represent a red spinner, the female spinner of some of the olives.

• Devised by Devon fly tier R. S. Austin about 1900, but named by G. E. M Skues, who was in regular correspondence with Austin.

• Perhaps JW's pattern and particularly the body may be preferable to some fly tiers that have difficulty in obtaining the correct dubbing mix for R. S. Austin's dressing of the fly. It is interesting to note that Alexander Mackintosh, as long ago as 1806 used wool from the ram's testicles in his Greendrake pattern (Alexander Mackintosh, *The Driffield Angler*, 1806).

Mike Reed's comments: I used the under covert feather from a starling's wing for this one. The pink Uni Micro tinsel body was a little darker than standard pink but looked good.

Blue Dun

HOOK: **13**

HACKLE: **A feather from the back of a woodhawk (sparrowhawk). It is a blue dun hackle which is just the right shade for this particular fly. The feather from a young lapwing will kill but the sparrowhawk hackle is preferred.**

BODY: **Light olive and yellow silk twisted to show in alternate bands.**

HEAD: **Loop of orange tinsel, or particularly in the autumn a loop of red tinsel, imitates the large eyes of the fly and adds to the attraction of this excellent killing pattern of the blue dun.**

Comments
• Large olive or blue dun (*Baetis vernus, B. tenax* or *B.buceratus*).
• According to Courtney Williams (1977), the large olive of spring is often known as the blue dun. As the season advances, the olive dun has a tendency to become lighter and smaller and the autumn insect does not compare in size with those of spring. The hatch usually starts up suddenly about midday and is generally over by late afternoon.
• The natural insect hatches in every month of the year, although only abundantly so in spring and autumn. The big hatches decrease towards the end of May when the trout transfer their affections to the iron-blue dun directly when that fly makes it appearance. By mid June the olive ceases to show in any strength, although it appears in large numbers again towards the end of August or early September. (Courtney Williams, 1977).
Mike Reed's comments: Use the feather from the leading edge of a coot wing, a natural blue dun. The eyes on this fly and others are made from a loop of Uni Micro tinsel or a thin piece of flat lurex; you might need a razor blade to cut wider lurex down.

Dark Watchet or Iron Blue Dun

The standard dressing of orange and purple silk dubbed with a little mole fur is a good killer, but I prefer the mulberry art silk ribbed with orange tying silk. After all, on examination of the natural fly, there is a fair amount of both orange and mulberry about the body and I think the mulberry shade cannot be bettered, especially when the art silk becomes rough, like dubbing, and the orange ribbing shows through. The dry pattern must have a dark blue Andalusian cock hackle of good quality.

HOOK: 16
HACKLE: Feather from a young cock jackdaw or from outside a young rook wing.
BODY: Mulberry artificial silk ribbed with orange tying silk.
HEAD: Blob of orange transparent varnish on the orange tying silk.

Comments
• The Dark Watchet is a pattern used to imitate the iron blue dun (*Baetis niger, B. muticus*) and purple dun (*Paraleptophlebia cinta*). This fly also is used to imitate the claret dun (*Leptophlebia vespertina*) on stillwaters. The natural iron blue dun hatches from April onwards. Pritt (1885) noted that the natural fly appears on Yorkshire rivers about the same time as the swallows first come, and the artificial fly will often kill well on cold days all through the season.

- This fly presents one of the most interesting examples of the blending of silks and well deserves Pritt's comment that it is, 'one of the daintiest morsels with which you can tempt a trout, and one of the most difficult to imitate satisfactorily'.
- Interesting to note that JW prefers to use mulberry artificial silk rather than purple tying silk and believes this shade to be more representative of the natural on the Wharfe.
- The word Watchet is thought to be of French origin, commonly used in the eighteenth century to describe cloth of a light blue colour. The term Watchet is therefore used to describe the light-blue/blue-grey shade of the hackles.
- Very old pattern, covered in Jackson's book *The Practical Fly-Fisher* (1854), however, he called this fly the Pigeon Blue Bloa.
- The Dark Watchet was included in Sylvester Lister's (1898) *List of Flies for the Wharfe*. Lister's pattern included as follows. Feather: from back of merlin hawk. Head: orange silk. Body: orange and purple silk twisted with a little mole's fur. Lister also remarked, 'a very small fly but a favourite on cold blustery days'.
- The Dark Watchet can also be tied with the smallest marginal feather from the coot wing.

Mike Reed's comments: Standard tying, the head varnish was a mix of orange and clear cellire.

Light Watchet

Dressed very fine and neatly, the fly-man won't have any trouble in catching a few trout when this fly appears. It very quickly changes into the spinner and it is in this guise that the angler will be troubled in dressing an imitation.

HOOK: 16
HACKLE: The Light Bloa feather from the fieldfare back.
BODY: Straw coloured silk.
HEAD: Straw silk.

Comments

- This pattern is supposed to imitate the metamorphosis of the young iron blue dun to the mature iron blue dun (*Baetis niger, B. muticus*). The Dark Watchet and Light Watchet patterns should be fished together as the naturals also appear at the same time. The natural iron blue dun hatches from April onwards. Pritt (1885) preferred to fish the Light Watchet on mild days and in the evening during the summer. Lister (1889) said the pattern was also suitable to imitate various olives (various *Baetis* species).

- This fly was also known as the Spinning Jenny, Pearl Drake or Little White Spinner (Jackson, 1854).
- It is not an easy fly to imitate and is a very delicate transparent insect; the lightest colour dun hackle should be used. Francis Walbran remarked in his 'notes' to Theakston that he never found the artificial killed well, and he knew one fly dresser in Yorkshire that had ceased to dress the fly because of his despair in his ability to produce an imitation of the natural fly to his satisfaction.
- The Light Watchet is included in Sylvester Lister's list of flies for the Wharfe (1889). His pattern included as follows. Feather: from the outside of the swallows wing. Body: straw coloured and gold tinsel. He also remarked that the Light Watchet should be fished at the same time as the Dark Watchet and commented that it was often taken better.
- Pritt's dressing of the Light Watchet included as follows. Wings: of a jay. Body: straw coloured silk. Legs: fibres from a yellow plover.
- A suitable alternative for the light bloa feather from the fieldfare back in JW's dressing is a pale starling feather hackle (Fogg, 1988).

Mike Reed's comments: Any bloa feather can be substituted with a starling hackle. Buy a whole skin for a whole range of blue/grey/ natural black colours from the body or wing.

Water Cricket (also called The Red Waterhen)

This fly is a good representation of the water cricket, often seen in action when iron blue duns are coming down the river, darting out from the bank and seizing the duns, and taking a heavier toll of the iron blue than the trout.

HOOK: 14.

HACKLE: Two turns of a hackle feather from the underside of a waterhen wing.

BODY: Red tinsel.

HEAD: One turn bronze peacock herl and one turn of red tinsel.

Dressing published in the Fishing Gazette, 1943, but did not appear in JW's notebook of wet fly dressings.

Comments

- Water cricket or sometimes called water measurer. Order – *Hemiptera*, Family – *Hydrometridae*, Genus – *Velia*, Species – *Currens*.
- This insect feeds upon small flies, etc. whose blood it sucks in a similar manner to that of the land spider. It runs upon the water, and darts upon its prey whilst struggling

on the surface. In the hot summer months it is provided with wings. This pattern can be fished in March and April, preferably when the iron blue dun is not very abundant on the water.

• The Water Cricket was developed by Alfred Ronalds who published the pattern in the *Fly-Fisher's Entomology* in 1836. The Water Cricket was also included in T. C. Hofland's *The British Angler's Manual*, (1839) and also within T. E. Pritt's *Yorkshire Trout Flies* (1885).

• Roger Fogg (1988) suggested that this pattern may be used as a weighted point fly on a traditional loch cast, or may be fished as a single deeply sunk nymph in a kind of sink-and-draw retrieve. It may be classed as a 'fancy' stillwater nymph which seems its best role.

Mike Reed's comments: Standard tying, use Uni Micro tinsel for the head.

Waterhen Bloa

This fly is the small dark olive of spring and autumn. Some tiers of flies recommend mole fur dubbing. This is altogether wrong as the body of the natural is of ivory shade.

HOOK: 14.

HACKLE: The spoon shaped feather from under the waterhen wing which are found on the bottom row of feathers.

BODY: Light yellow silk dubbed with almost white fur from the belly of the hare or from the blue fox rabbit underbelly.

HEAD: Yellow silk.

Comments

• The Waterhen Bloa is a version of the old Blue Dun dressing and whilst principally intended as an imitation of the large dark olive (*Baetis rhodani*) it will work as a general imitation of many *ephemera* nymphs and emerging creatures – small dark olives (*Baetis Scambus*), medium olives or blue dun (*Baetis vernus, B. tenax, B. buceratus*). It is one of the best flies to have on the cast in spring when the large dark olive (also known as the large spring olive) nymph is present in the water. Ask any North Country wet-fly fishermen to name their favourite list of North Country patterns and I bet few would leave out the Waterhen Bloa.

• The Waterhen Bloa is one of the best examples of blending silks and furs in order to achieve a natural insect's colour or shade. JW's dressing is unconventional but does show that he was concerned with trying to match his artificial to the insects he found on the River Wharfe. However, flies with bodies of yellow silk sparsely dubbed with mole fur have been successfully used on the Wharfe for many years (and definitely preferred by Eric H. Wright – Bradford Waltonians).

• Many of the old Waterhen Bloa dressings use an under covert feather from the waterhen or moorhen, however, some tiers prefer the dark grey feather from the marginal coverts or bow of the wing. Similar feathers from the coot or starling may be used, and it is as well to remember that the amendments to the Wildlife and Countryside Act may make traditional feathers difficult to procure.

• The feather used for the hackle should possess fibres which are a little longer than the hook shank. The word 'bloa' relates to the colour of the sky when rain and storms seem imminent; therefore a feather of an inky-grey shade should be used.

• In tying this fly, Pritt would have used the 'bloa' or 'blae' feather from the waterhen under coverts. Some tiers suggest this is too light for the Waterhen Bloa and a darker feather should be used to dress the Blue Dun. It is possible that Pritt's and JW's pattern was tied to resemble a lighter fly in order to generally imitate paler ephemeroptera. In this case a waterhen under covert feather and dubbing of lighter fur from the blue rabbit under fur is preferable.

• Some tiers use a well waxed primrose tying silk (Pearsall's shade 3). Tiers using nylon threads rather than silks can achieve the correct olive-yellow shade by rubbing the thread sparingly with Mucilin grease rather than wax. This also adds the right kind of thickness which is an aid to the dubbing of fur.

• It is vitally important that the dubbing must be very sparsely applied so that when the fur is twirled onto the thread the yellow is still visible through the dubbing. An inch or so of dubbed fur is sufficient.

• Many tiers incorporate a small thorax formed by a little ball of fur just behind the hackle. Apart from creating the natural insects profile, this also provides a functional addition to the fly, because when the hackle is wound close to the thorax, it enables the fibres to take a more upright 'set' and gives them more 'kick' and movement. Arguably, many standard patterns are improved in this manner.

• Very useful fly in September and beyond for grayling.

Mike Reed's comments: Standard tying.

Hackled Olive Dun

A good fly in May on the Yorkshire rivers. Contemporary with a fly named Fieldfare Bloa, which is the wet winged pattern.

HOOK: 14

HACKLE: Feather from under the coot or a young sparrowhawk wing.

BODY: Light olive tying silk and a strand of yellow artificial silk twisted and wrapped on to show in alternate bands.

HEAD: Two turns of orange silk.

Dressing published in the Fishing Gazette, 1943, but did not appear in JW's notebook of wet fly dressings.

Comments

- Olive Dun (*Baetis rhodani, B. vernu*s). Most common of the *Ephemeridae*.
- Hatches every month of the year and abundantly in spring and autumn.
- Woolley recommended the addition of a gold tip to the bodies of all wet olive duns.

Mike Reed's comments: Standard tying.

Winter Brown

The body may be made of red bronze peacock herl and ribbed with orange tinsel. This is similar to one of Bradshaw's dressings which, was ribbed with orange silk. The orange tinsel, however, adds attraction which is sometimes necessary.

HOOK: 14.

HACKLE: A well marked hackle from under the woodcock wing which shows grey and white.

BODY: Orange silk, not too bright orange, ribbed with orange tinsel.

THORAX: Peacock herl.

HEAD: Peacock herl.

Comments

- Pattern used to imitate *Nemoura meyeri*, one of the minor *perlidae* (stoneflies). Similar in appearance to the February red (*Taeniopteryx nebulosa*), but smaller.
- This dressing appears to be the same as Theakston's (1853) Early Brown. Theakston recommended its use from the beginning of February to the end of April. The Winter Brown or Early Brown, together with the Light Woodcock, Dark Woodcock, Orange Woodcock, Brown Owl and the Needle flies are patterns to imitate various species of *perlidae*, which occur in the early spring. The Winter Brown is a useful dressing used to resemble any small member of the stonefly family which the angler is unable to identify with any degree of exactitude. The *Nemoura* family are very common and when a breeze carries them on to the water, fish take them readily.
- Included in T. E. Pritt's book *North Country Flies* (1886). Pritt said this fly was 'a favourite fly on all the Yorkshire rivers, killing well on wild, windy days in March

and April. The wings assume a lighter shade in the course of ten days after its first appearance on the water when it is commonly dressed as the Little Winter Brown or Light Woodcock.' Also included in Edmonds and Lee *Brook and River Trouting* (1916) as a fly to be fished in March and April.
• John Turton in the *Anglers Manual* (1836) preferred to use the Winter Brown as a grayling fly for October and November fishing.
Mike Reed's comments: Standard tying, use a strand of orange flashabou or varnished fluo. Orange floss strands for the rib.

Hackled Yellow Sally

This fly lasts for three months on the Yorkshire Wharfe: May, June and July. The statements in some angling books regarding it not being relished by trout and not generally taken by them are pure nonsense. The above dressing will kill trout throughout the months mentioned.

HOOK: 14.
HACKLE: Underwing feather from a young starling, or a hooded crow neck feather.
BODY: Green-olive and yellow silk twisted and wrapped onto the hook shank to show in alternate ribs, then rib with four turns of yellow tinsel.
THORAX: Blue fox rabbit fur dyed in a yellow dye to give a green-olive dubbing.
HEAD: Twisted green-olive and yellow silk.

Dressing published in the Fishing Gazette, 1943, but did not appear under that name in JW's notebook of wet fly dressings.

Comments
• Dressing to resemble the yellow sally stonefly (*Isoperla grammatica*). This is a medium-sized stonefly which is easily recognisable by its yellow body and yellow-green wings. The length of the adult varies from 8-13mm. The adults appear on the water from April to August, but mainly between May and June on hot days.
• Included in Alfred Ronalds' *The Fly-Fisher's Entomology* (1836). Ronalds' dressing included wings from a wing feather of a white hen or fieldfare stained pale yellow.
• Jackson's (1854) dressing included: silk – yellow; body – yellow silk ribbed with fawn silk; wings – pale yellow dyed feather; hackle – yellow hen hackle feather.
• JW obviously disagrees with Pritt's statement that this fly 'rarely kills well, and that the natural insect does not appear to be much relished by trout'. However, it should be noted that Pritt's dressing included wings from a green linnet's tail. JW's hackled

dressing is quite different from Ronald's, Jackson's and Pritt's winged versions. Perhaps JW's dressing fished just below the surface film provides a good pattern to imitate the yellow sally nymph. The nymph seems to prefer moderately fast water up to three feet deep. As with other stone flies, this nymph crawls out of the water before the winged adult emerges. Winged flies can sometimes be seen beneath submerged stones in fast flowing shallow water.

• Interesting to note that the Yellow Sally was not included in Sylvester Lister's list of flies for the River Wharfe (1898).

Mike Reed's comments: Standard tying. A fine gold tinsel rib instead of yellow could be used, or varnished yellow floss strands give a nice effect.

Blue Partridge

This fly, which comes out in July, must not be confused with the Gravel Bed Spider. It is an upright wing fly which changes into a spinner a few days after the appearance of the dun stage. The wings assume a transparency, the legs which were red/ black go to normal red. The body changes to blue ultramarine and what do we see but the Broughton Point of course. The hackle may be pulled up for a single wing copy of the dun.

HOOK: 13

HACKLE: The freckled feather, fairly large, from the partridge, one of medium brown freckle.

BODY: Blue heron herl.

THORAX: Peacock herl.

HEAD: Peacock herl.

Comments

• One of T. E. Pritt's patterns; he noted this fly to be 'a first rate killer in a biggish water any time after the middle of May'.

• This fly was included in the list of artificial flies used by Sylvester Lister Snr., Barden Tower, near Bolton Abbey (1898). He also called the Blue Partridge a 'Gravel Bed Spider' (*Hexatoma fuscipennis*), which conflicts with JW. Lister's pattern which included the speckled feather (bluish) from the partridge back or silver pheasant. Head – magpie herl. Body – light blue covered with heron's herl. Lister said this fly comes on early in May, often kills well on bright days to end of July.

• Alfred Ronalds' (1836) Gravel Bed was also referred to as the Spider Fly or Sand Gnat (order – *Diptera*, family – *Tipulidae*, genus – *Anisomera*, species – *obscura*). If the Blue Partridge was not to be confused with the Gravel Bed Spider, perhaps JW's pattern is an imitation of the sand gnat? Ronalds' pattern included as follows. Body: lead coloured thread. Hackle: dark dun cock's hackle or bright outside feather of woodcock wing. Wings: from under covert feather of the woodcock wing. Legs: black cock's hackle wound twice round the body.

Mike Reed's comments: The heron can be substituted with the grey primary feather from a coot wing.

Dry fly patterns

* Published in the *Fishing Gazette*.

Olive Quill

Use in spring and autumn months.

HOOK: 13

HACKLE: **Blue Andalusian cock.**

BODY: **Peacock quill.**

Comments

• The blue Andalusian cock hackle, appended to the description as an example, is a typical blue dun hackle with dun tips to the fibres, which becomes blue-grey towards the quill. This is the first of many examples to suggest that JW's ideas for dry flies had been strongly influenced by Halford (1886, 1910).

• JW's pattern for the Olive Quill illustrates the problem of relating the nomenclature to the patterns given in reference books. An Olive Quill according to authorities such as Veniard (1964) and Roberts (1995) has a tail of medium olive cock fibres, a body of peacock quill dyed olive and a medium olive hackle.

• Olive dun/spinner (*Cloeon dipterum*). Emergence during the day throughout the summer, with peaks in June, July and September. Useful in the late afternoon and evening.

Mike Reed comment: Standard hackle tying, the peacock quill body comes from the blue section in the eye feather.

Greenwell's Glory

Use in spring and autumn months.

HOOK: 14

HACKLE: Dark blue Andalusian cock.

BODY: **Green olive fur (dyed opossum fur).**

RIB: **Yellow tinsel.**

Comments

• The example of the hackle provided for this pattern is another blue-dun hackle but darker than the feather recommended for the Olive Quill.

• JW's hackled pattern bears little resemblance to the familiar Greenwell/Wright/Brown winged pattern, with its characteristic well waxed yellow silk body and Coch-y-bondhu hackle (James Wright of Sprouston 1829-1902). One can only assume that it was JW's creation for use on the Wharfe when the smokey-blue spring olive, blue winged olive and dark olive dun naturals are on the water (and when the wet pattern of the Waterhen Bloa is also appropriate).

• Courtney Williams in his *Dictionary of Trout Flies* (1950) describes a hackled version of a Greenwell, which has a double hackle of furnace cock and medium blue dun cock, and comments that 'the hackled version is becoming increasingly popular, and I must confess a great liking for it'.

• Medium olive dun/spinner (*Baetis vernus*, *B. tenax* and *B. buceratus*). Emergence during the day or early evening throughout the summer, with a peak in May and June. Hatches are often heavy.

• This pattern also works well on still waters when olive-bodied flies are hatching.

Mike Reed's comment: I could not find any yellow tinsel. I tried yellow flashabou strands for ribbing but it didn't look right. The best effect was achieved by using Uni-floss strands dipped in varnish. This makes a super rib that I have since used on other patterns. Jim Wynn liked varnished bodies so I hope he would approve. Opposum fur was substituted with dyed white rabbit.

Medium Olive

Use in May and June.

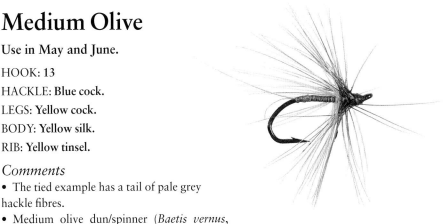

HOOK: **13**
HACKLE: **Blue cock.**
LEGS: **Yellow cock.**
BODY: **Yellow silk.**
RIB: **Yellow tinsel.**

Comments

• The tied example has a tail of pale grey hackle fibres.

• Medium olive dun/spinner (*Baetis vernus*, *B. tenax* and *B. buceratus*). Emergence during the day or early evening throughout the summer, with a peak in May and June. Hatches are often heavy.

• The medium olive is one of the most important flies of early summer. Hatches usually begin in the late morning and continue into the afternoon and early evening, with duns emerging in steady trickles rather than batches. Sometimes the resulting fall of spinners can be dense enough to cause a selective evening rise.

Mike Reed's comments: Again I used the varnished floss for the rib. Tying two hackles in is something I do quite a lot. If you wind a long hen hackle first and then a genetic cock hackle through it, you end up with a super buoyant fly that looks very natural and leggy.

Light Olive

Use in May and June.

HOOK: **14**
HACKLE: **Grey dun cock.**
LEGS: **Naples yellow cock.**
BODY: **Yellow silk.**

Comments

• Olive upright dun/spinner (*Rithrogena semicolorata*). Emergence sometimes in early morning, but more normally from early afternoon through almost to dusk. It occurs throughout the summer, but the peak hatches are from mid-May to mid-July.

• Water temperature can greatly affect the rate of development and their hatching period can vary significantly from year to year depending on the weather.

• During heavy hatches trout can be totally preoccupied with these flies and a close imitation is the only way of getting results.

Mike Reed's comments: Hard to be certain what Jim Wynn meant by grey, but I guessed there wouldn't be much blue in it. Naples yellow is again open to debate, so my conclusion was to head for the mustard end of the spectrum.

Blue Winged Olive

Use in June and July.

HOOK: **13**
HACKLE: **Luminous grey cock.**
BODY: **Yellow silk or nylon.**
RIB: **Gold tinsel.**

Comments

• Blue winged olive dun (*Ephemerella ignita*). Hatches are often large, usually beginning in late evening towards the end of May and continuing to the end of September. They tend to occur earlier, sometimes during the day, as the season progresses.

• This is a medium-largish fly with blue-grey wings, three pronounced tails and an olive coloured body.

• After mating, the female spinners may be seen flying upstream in large swarms, each fly with her large green egg-ball tucked beneath her tail. Favoured egg laying sites for this species seem to be the faster, shallower stretches lined with gravel or coarse sand.

• It is understandable that such a common fly has been imitated countless times in fur and feather, under many names, and has given rise to much discussion in angling literature as to the best dressing. It is not an easy fly to imitate. The perfect pattern that rose trout after trout yesterday is just as likely to be totally ignored today, and one is hard-put to pin down the reason.

Mike Reed's comments: I struggled with luminous grey, and ended up putting a small amount of yellow dye in with the grey. The gold tinsel rib was gold flashabou strands which looked fine on this pattern.

Orange Quill

This is the blue winged olive spinner for use in the evening during June, July and August. It is also a good grayling fly in the autumn.

HOOK: 14

HACKLE: Medium blue dyed cock.

LEGS: Luminous orange cock.

BODY: Orange dyed quill.

Comments

• The tied example has a tail of orange cock fibres.

• Blue winged olive dun (*Ephemerella ignita*). Hatches are often large, usually beginning in late evening towards the end of May and continuing to the end of September.

• Although the body of this dun appears yellow-green, and has been likened to a ripening greengage, it was discovered by accident that the Orange Quill was very successful when blue winged olive duns were hatching. This appears to be strange when the bright-orange body of the artificial is compared with the drab, greenish body of the natural. However, the true colour of the body is in fact orange, but is overlaid with a slatey-blue integument and appears to our eyes as yellow-green. The eye of the fish probably relegates the blue and green into an unseen background, so that to the fish, the body appears as a distinct orange.

• G. E. M. Skues in the 1890s was responsible for popularising the Orange Quill, which is a good approximation of the female blue winged olive spinner, also commonly called the sherry spinner.

• C. F. Walker provides a good winged dressing for the Olive Quill.

Mike Reed's comments: Again that luminous dye was specified, and Veniard's do a Fluoro Orange that must be similar.

Iron Blue Dun – Male

HOOK: 15

HACKLE: Dyed iron blue cock.

BODY: Orange and purple silk twisted and dubbed with mole fur.

Comments

• Iron blue dun (*Baetis niger* and *B. muticus*). Emergence at the surface during the day. Hatches are sometimes prolific (but seldom regular) throughout the summer, with peaks in May and September.

• Some hatches may take place in spring depending on the weather conditions.

• The iron blue dun is a small upwing fly. It is much darker than any of the other upwing flies, and its wings are a very dark grey.

• The natural fly has a body that ranges from a very dark-brown olive to a greyish black. The wings are of a greyish-blue colour, while the tails are a dark grey. Legs show a distinct olive-brown colour.

• This fly still appears in cold wet and windy weather.

Mike Reed's comments: The twisted silk body no doubt came from the Dark Watchet tying. It's hard to put too little mole dub on this. Using Pearsalls Gossamer silks is essential when tying this type of body, because the colours and appearance are perfect. Leave a small tag undubbed.

Iron Blue Dun – Female

These two flies (male and female) are always on the water together in the later part of April onwards. Difficult to know which are being taken, so should try both.

HOOK: 15

HACKLE: Very light blue cock.

BODY: Coates lemon yellow terylene thread.

Comment

• Iron blue dun (*Baetis niger* and *B. muticus*). Emergence at the surface during the day. Hatches are sometimes prolific (but seldom regular) throughout the summer, with peaks in May and September.

• The iron blue dun emerges at the surface in open water, and has the reputation of hatching in bad weather; however, on many rivers the hatches can be fairly dense even on spring sunny days. Specific imitations have been devised, but a general pattern is often acceptable in the rough and tumble of a spring spate river.

• The female iron blue dun is slightly larger and stouter in the body than the male. They also possess a pale olive-yellow eye and do not have claspers appended to the penultimate segment of the abdomen.

Mike Reed's comments: This is a simple tying that would kill on most waters, and I will be trying some on our Hebridean trout. The body was made from strands of Uni-Glo floss, 600 denier phosphorescent white. Take a length and knot each end before dyeing; I normally use Dylon, but the Veniard dyes are good for the dun and grey colours.

Small Red Spinner

Sometimes taken when the iron blue dun is on the water.

HOOK: **14**

HACKLE: **Dark blue Andalusian cock.**

BODY: **Cock pheasant tail herl.**

RIB: **Gold wire.**

TAIL: **Three strands of cock hackle fibres.**

Comments

• This dressing is for the spinner of the small dark olive, also known as the July dun (*Baetis scambus*). This pattern may also be taken as the autumn spinner (*Ecdyonurus dispar*). This species is common and well distributed on rivers throughout the country.

• The spinners may be seen from early evening from July to early October, but the peak hatches are during August and September. However, the fly can be seen as early as February and as late as November on some rivers. It is seldom seen on the water in quantity.

• The female spinner crawls under the surface to deposit her eggs. Trout feed upon the spent spinners, which after laying their eggs are unable to break through the surface film and become trapped below or within it. The possibility of fish feeding on these should not be overlooked if floating duns and spinners are being refused by feeding fish.

Mike Reed's comments: Standard tying, pretty much a Pheasant Tail.

Dark Olive Spinner

Use anytime after hatches of medium olives.

HOOK: 13

HACKLE: Medium olive cock.

LEGS: Red cock.

BODY: Cock pheasant tail herl.

RIB: Orange tinsel.

Comments

• The tied example has a tail of three cock fibres.

• Dark olive spinner (*Baetis rhodani, B. atrebatinus*). Hatches occur during the day from October to early May. They are seldom seen on the water in sufficient quantities. This is because the species is an early-season one and our spring weather is seldom warm enough in the evening to favour swarming, so mating takes place during the day as and when the opportunity occurs.

• The female spinner has transparent wings. The upper abdomen is dark reddish brown with pale rings and the lower abdomen is light olive. The legs are of brown-olive and the two tails grey-olive with feint red rings.

Mike Reed's comments: Again that pleasing double hackle and varnished floss rib.

Blue Winged Olive Spinner

Sometimes taken in preference to an Olive Quill.

HOOK: 13

HACKLE: Blue Andalusian cock.

BODY: Rusty red fur.

RIB: Gold wire.

Comments

• The tied example has a tail of three grey cock hackle fibres.

• Blue winged olive spinner (*Ephemerella ignita*). This is probably the commonest of the upwinged flies. Hatches are often large, usually beginning in late evening towards the end of May and continuing to the end of September. They tend to occur earlier, sometimes during the day, as the season progresses.

• The female spinner is commonly referred to as the

sherry spinner. The female spinner is distinctive with its little green ball-like egg-sac carried at the rear of the abdomen. The wings are transparent with pale brown veins and the body varies from olive-brown to sherry-red. The legs are pale brown and tails are olive-grey with light brown rings.
• The male spinner is one of the few that are of interest to trout and grayling. The wings are transparent with light brown veins and the abdomen is dark or rich brown. The legs are pale brown and the three tails are fawn with black rings.
• This fly is difficult to imitate successfully; also try Olive Quill and Orange Quill.

Mike Reed's comments: A simple hackle tying, using two turns of hackle for a calm water pattern, or more to make a more buoyant job for fast water work. The rusty red fur comes from a rabbit skin. Buy a whole skin so you get a large range of colours from white to natural red.

Pheasant Tail Spinner

Of all the spinners, this is the one to use at any time you are in doubt as to what to put on!

HOOK: 14
HACKLE: **Honey dun cock.**
BODY: **Cock pheasant tail herl.**
RIB: **Gold wire.**
TAIL: **Three strands of hackle fibres.**

Comments
• A good pattern to represent most of the spinners is a Pheasant Tail Spinner, including the following:
Turkey brown spinner (*Paraleptophlebia submarginata*). Emergence in day time in May and June, in ones or twos.
Claret spinner (*Leptophlebia vespertina*). Emergence during the day from early May to early June.
Sepia spinner (*Leptophlebia marginata*). Emergence during the middle of the day in April and early May, but hatches are usually rather sparse.
Blue winged olive spinner (*Ephemerella ignita*). Emergence late evenings towards the end of May to September.
Autumn spinner (*Ecdyonurus dispar*). Emergence early evenings from July to early October.
Large brook spinner (*Ecdyonurus torrentis*). Hatches tend to be sparse and occur during the day or early evening from late March to July.
March brown spinner (*Rithrogena germanica*). Hatches, where they do occur, are often

on a grand scale during the middle of the day in March, April and early May. Most trout seem to feed on the nymphs just below the surface as they are about to emerge.

Medium olive spinner (*Baetis vernus, B. tenax* and *B. buceratus*). Emergence during the day or early evening throughout the summer, with peak in May and June. Hatches are often heavy.

Small dark olive spinner (*Baetis scambus*). Emergence from mid-day to late evening. The spinners occur from June until November, with a peak in July and August. Hatches are substantial and prolonged.

Iron blue spinner (*Baetis niger* and *B. muticus*). Emergence during the day throughout the summer, with peaks in May and September. Hatches are sometimes prolific but seldom regular.

Lake olive spinner (*Cloeon similie*). Emergence during the day throughout the summer, with peaks in May and June and again in August and September.

Ditch spinner (*Habrophlebia fusca*). Emergence from May to September.

Dusky Yellowstreak (*Heptagenia lateralis*). Emergence is from May to September.

Mike Reed's comments: A lighter tying of the Small Red Spinner.

Great Red Spinner

Use from March to August.

HOOK: 13, long shank

HACKLE: Dark, grizzled-blue Andalusian cock.

BODY: Maroon silk.

RIB: Orange tinsel.

THORAX: Peacock herl.

Comments

• JW's tied example had a tail of grey cock fibres.

• Female spinner of the Autumn dun or August dun (*Ecdyonurus dispar*). Also may be used to represent the late March brown female spinner (*Ecdyonurus venosus*). Hatches of the August/Autumn dun appear from June to October with peaks in July and September. The late March brown is more common than the March brown. The adults emerge from April to June, and sometimes in August and September.

• The female spinner of the August/Autumn dun has transparent wings with dark brown veins. The abdomen is reddish-brown with a darker underside. The two long tails are dark brown and the legs are olive-brown. The male spinner is of little interest.

• The female spinner of the late March brown is larger and has a redder body than the male. The female spinner can also be imitated by the Cinnamon Quill.

• The great red spinner is seldom seen on the Wharfe in great numbers, but it must make a juicy mouthful for a trout.

Mike Reed's comments: A real one off tying. Peacock herl thoraxes and heads are well used on Yorkshire soft-hackled patterns – the eye feather gives the ideal sized strand on most occasions. The orange tinsel was strands of varnished Uni-Neon floss Hot Orange.

Silver Sedge

A very good fly indeed, especially on the River Nidd. Good for grayling.

HOOK: 14

HACKLE: Ginger cock, well spread.

BODY: Silver tinsel.

TAG: Luminous orange wool.

Comments

• Small silver sedge (*Odontocerum albicorne*, *Lepidostoma hirtum*). This is a fairly large species (approximate anterior wing-length 13-18mm) with reddish brown eyes, and is found only in fairly fast-flowing water, with a preference for a stony bottom.

• Emergence June to October during day and evening in open water. This fly is particularly useful during the evenings in summer and early autumn.

• The silver or grey sedge has silvery grey wings (often with black striate marks in the centre), and tend to have a yellowish tinge with age. It has a grey body, long toothed antennae and long hairy maxillary palps.

• The Silver Sedge is a good imitation of the many small, light-coloured sedges of summer, but it also serves as a general sedge pattern for the River Wharfe.

• The Silver Sedge is a useful autumn grayling pattern for the River Wharfe.

• Possibly could be tied without the orange tag for use as a sedge pattern for trout in the summer. The orange tag would appear to be a good pattern for the grayling in autumn.

Mike Reed's comments: Veniard's Fluorescent Orange wool for the tail. I tied the palmered hackle in at the head, wound it to the tail and secured it with a silver wire rib. Jim Wynn doesn't mention the rib, so the hackle could be tied in at the tail by the tip and wound to the head. I prefer the first method.

Pale Watery Dun

Use on summer evenings.

HOOK: 16
HACKLE: Off white cock.
BODY: Lemon yellow silk or nylon.

Comments

- The tied example has a tail of three matching cock hackle fibres.
- Pale watery (*Baetis fuscatus*). Emergence during the day from May to October.
- In the past, several species of flies were called pale wateries. This group included the small spurwing, the large spurwing and the pale evening dun. The dressing provided will provide a suitable pattern to imitate all these flies.
- The fly has medium or pale grey wings and a pale greyish-olive body, of which the last two segments are pale yellow. The legs are light olive and the two tails grey. The yellow eyes of the male help to identify it.
- The Funneldun by Neil Patterson is also a very good pattern to imitate the pale watery dun. A key feature of the Funneldun is the forward-sloping hackle, which is funnelled out over the bulky thorax. A small V is cut from the underside of the hackle, and this ensures that the fly lands hook point in the air every time it is cast.
- The pale watery dun is greedily taken by grayling as well as trout. We have caught numerous trout with this pattern on the Wharfe at Otley during June.

Mike Reed's comments: Standard tying.

Tups Indispensable

Very good evening fly, taken well after sunset when there is still a pink glow on the water.

HOOK: 16
HACKLE: Pale honey dun.
BODY: Half pink luminous silk dubbing, tail half of yellow silk.
TAIL: Three matching cock hackle fibres.

Comments

- Small male spurwing spinner: R. A. Austin tied the Tups to represent the red spinner, the female spinner of some of the olives. Today it is probably fished as a copy of a pale watery spinner (*Baetis fuscatus*) and small male spurwing spinner (*Centroptilum luteolum*). This is an early season species and its spinners are often responsible for the evening rises as weather and water warm up towards the end of May.

• The pale watery male spinners, in particular, swarm close to the water and are often blown on to the surface, where the trout take them readily. It is one of the few species of which it pays to have a copy of the male spinner.

• Fly originally devised by R. S. Austin about 1890. The Tups has become a popular fly, fished either wet or dry. Some anglers use it when the trout are on the *Caenis* (the anglers' curse); fished on sizes 14 or 16, either as a static dry fly or retrieved an inch at a time on fine leaders.

• JW's fly does not use the traditional dubbing material devised by Austin and later modified by Skues.

• Use a slightly larger hook size to represent the large spurwing spinner (*Centoptilum pennulatum*).

Mike Reed's comments: The luminous pink dub used was Veniard Fluorescent Wool – the fibres can be teased out and then dubbed.

Badger Midge

Very good fly when trout are taking midges. Good for grayling.

HOOK: **16**

HACKLE: **Badger cock, very small (example of feather in notebook is only 25mm total length with hackle fibres of 15mm!).**

BODY: **Black tinsel with silver tip.**

THORAX: **Black ostrich herl**

Comments

• Emerging midge pupae (*Chironomidae*). Probably represents a black midge. Period of emergence: May–June and August–September. Calm water is favoured for a hatch and the evenings of hot sunny days often have the largest hatches.

• Pupae vary in size and colour and often have a pronounced bend to their segmented body. They have whitish breathing filaments at the head and whitish appendages to the tail to aid swimming. The rising or emerging pupae under the surface film are of the most interest to trout. The adults may emerge fairly speedily, or may take up to a couple of hours, hanging just below the surface. Their movement is slow and may be in a horizontal plane or a slow rising and sinking for short distances. Some remain static with their breathing filaments suspended from the surface film. The thorax splits and the adult emerges, leaving its pupal case behind.

Mike Reed's comments: Super little fly. Use herl from the tip of the ostrich feather, the finest. Black tinsel would be a useful material, let me know where to buy some! I used varnished black silk.

Grey Duster

Said to be taken for the mayfly spent gnat, but I
have never done much good with it myself!

HOOK: 13

HACKLE: Badger cock

BODY: Blue/white rabbit fur dubbed onto
brown silk.

Comments

• Ronald Broughton (1898) suggests that the body
should contain a mixture of rabbit guard hairs from
the back and a little blue fur from under the white hair of the belly.

• Michael Leighton (quoted by Broughton, 1989) suggests that the body should have
a pinch of hare's fur added to the rabbit.

• Eric Wright strongly recommends his Grey Duster adaptation for the Wharfe
especially when the dark watchet is emerging on the water. The dressing is the Grey
Duster of JW, though he prefers to use mole fur for the dubbing, with an additional
dark red cock hackle dressed through the badger hackle.

• This is thought to be a general fly pattern to imitate a number of species including
the small spurwing dun (*Centroptilum luteolum*). Its size can be varied, therefore the
pattern can be used to imitate larger flies such as a medium olive (*Baetis vernus*), or
others as small as a pale watery (*Baetis fuscatus*). For general use through May to
September.

• John Goddard said the Grey Duster was an excellent general fly and the dressing
could be used to imitate the following:

Small spurwing dun (*Centroptilum luteolum*) – May through to September.

Needle fly (*Leuctra fusca*) – August to October.

Gravel bed fly (*Hexatoma fusipennis*) – late summer.

Water ermine (*Spilosoma urticae*) – white moth present in June. Also use the Ermine
Moth dressing on such occasions.

• One of Courtney Williams' most favoured flies. Donald Overfield said, 'On rivers
the length and breadth of the country I have found the Grey Duster to be an excellent
fly, frequently doing the trick when so-called imitations of the natural fly on the water
have been totally ignored. Yes, a truly favourite fly.'

Mike Reed's comments: Again having a whole rabbit skin helps. Pinch the white and
grey underfur in one go to get the right mix, not too much.

Little Mariott Fly

Just as good as the Pale Watery Dun.
Good evening fly and extra good for
grayling in the autumn.

HOOK: 16
HACKLE: Light blue cock.
BODY: Yellow silk dubbed with buff
opossum fur.

Comments

• The tied example has a tail of three matching cock hackle fibres.
• One must assume that this is a version of G. S. Marryat's fly (Little Marryat) but lacking the wings (Halford, 1889). The Little Marryat was devised by G. S. Marryat to be fished as a pale watery dun and spurwing imitation.
• Skues suggested cream seal fur for the body (Skues, 1921).
• Pale watery (*Baetis fuscatus*). Emergence during the day from May to October. Hatches are sometimes heavy.

Mike Reed's comments: The buff fur again comes from that rabbit skin; dub lightly so the silk rib shows through.

Orange Tups

One of my own creations; very
good throughout the summer
and autumn months.

Dressing as for Tups Indispensable
but with the pink dubbing replaced
by luminous Fiesta-orange.

Comments

• Small female spurwing spinner (little amber spinner) (*Centroptilum luteolum*). This is an early season species and its spinners are often responsible for the evening rises as weather and water warm up towards the end of May.
• The Orange Tups is possibly tied to represent the female spurwing spinner, commonly called the little amber spinner. The fly has dark brown eyes and, when fully spent, the top half of the body is a lovely pale amber colour, ringed cream.

Mike Reed's comments: Use Orange Veniard Fluorescent wool teased and dubbed.

Ginger Quill

A good general fly anytime during the season.

HOOK: 16
HACKLE: Light blue cock.
LEGS: Ginger cock.
BODY: Peacock quill.
TAIL: Three matching cock hackle fibres.

Comments

• This is a general fly for representing pale watery/lighter medium olive duns (*Baetis fuscatus*/*B. rhodani*). Also imitation of *B. binoculatus* and *B. scambus*. Period of emergence on hot days late June to August from midday to evening.

• There are two shades of olives, the dark and medium olives. The latter is considerably lighter; this would appear to be a pattern to imitate the lighter coloured medium olive. The necessity of observing the colour of fly which fish are taking will be appreciated as it will be a decisive factor when selecting an artificial pattern.

• The dun quickly becomes airborne, so an emerging pattern such as JW's pattern is often desirable.

• Use stripped peacock quill from the eye part of the feather.

• The Ginger Quill can be fished wet or dry and is a useful pattern for rivers and stillwater.

Mike Reed's comments: Standard tying. Soak the quill in water for an hour or two, this will help stop them breaking.

Orange Sedge

Just as good as the Silver Sedge; very good on reservoirs too.

HOOK: 14
HACKLE: Brown ginger cock.
BODY: Orange tinsel.
TAG: Luminous orange wool.

Comments

• This is possibly a variant of the cinnamon sedge (*Limnephilus lunatus*). This is one of the earliest of the more common species and, with ts distinctive mottled wings, one of the easiest sedges to recognise. The body varies from orange, orange/brown to green. The wings (14-15mm) are narrow and vary in colour from yellow to an orange/brown or cinnamon/brown with irregular brown patches and a distinctive pale lunate patch at the apex of the wings.

• This fly is very similar to the caperer. The caperer has mottled yellowish-brown wings and a body orangey-brown in colour.

• Its distribution is widespread and abundant. Emergence in late May to November during the day and early evening, close to emergent vegetation.

Mike Reed's comments: Standard tying.

Red Tag

September for trout and grayling; also in October and November for grayling, chub and dace.

HOOK: **14**
HACKLE: **Red cock.**
BODY: **Green peacock herl.**
TAG: **Red wool.**

Comments

• Max Walbran is perhaps best known for popularising the Red Tag in Yorkshire, this fly was shown to him by a Worcester angler who was visiting the River Ure in 1878. According to Courtney Williams the fly originated in Worcestershire in the 1850s and was known as the Worcester Gem.

• In the past the Red Tag has been primarily a river fly and a grayling pattern that catches thousands of grayling every autumn. Its coloration is similar to that of a Worm Fly, a pattern which does well early season when fished deep-down on the reservoirs. Now the Red Tag has a growing reputation as a top or centre dropper fly. The fly can be fished wet or dry.

• A tip from Reg Righyni (1968) on the tying of the tag of the dry fly is worth remembering. He tied the tag on the long side initially; if the grayling are well on the take, the longer tag helps the fly float correctly. If the fish are choosy, the tag can be clipped shorter.

• Some Yorkshire grayling fishers use a pattern with a lime-green tag, known as the Green Tag. The pattern with a crimson tag is known as the Crimson Tag, and that with a white floss or wool tag is the White Tag. The Gold Tag, which has a tip of gold tinsel, was once a popular fly.

• As with the Treacle Parkin and Orange Tag, the Red Tag is thought to imitate a beetle.

Mike Reed's comments: Standard tying. Use normal wool for the tag.

Honey Dun Bumble

A very excellent grayling fly. I remember one day in October, a member fishing Farfield Hall water for a good fish rising under a wooded slope. The member tried all he had to lure the fish without success. I gave him a copy of this fly which was taken first cast.

HOOK: 14

HACKLE: Light honey dun cock
(shoulder hackle only).

BODY: Peacock herl (green).

RIB: Pink tinsel.

TAG: Luminous pink silk.

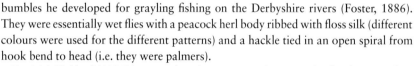

Comments

• The Honey Dun Bumble was David Foster's favourite from a series of five bumbles he developed for grayling fishing on the Derbyshire rivers (Foster, 1886). They were essentially wet flies with a peacock herl body ribbed with floss silk (different colours were used for the different patterns) and a hackle tied in an open spiral from hook bend to head (i.e. they were palmers).

• Fredrick Halford (1886) improved on these patterns for use as dry flies by using floss silk (only one or two strands) for the body and ribbing with a single strand of peacock sword. The various patterns had bodies of different coloured floss (e.g. claret, orange, yellow, pearl, purple, steely blue etc.) but all had an open spiral of cock hackle with two close turns at the head. Neither of the two series of Bumbles was dressed with a coloured tag.

• In contrast the Witches, created by Rolt (1901) were given a red ibis or scarlet dyed swan tag, but resembled Foster's Bumbles in having a peacock herl body ribbed with fine gold tinsel and light honey dun palmered hackle.

• Jim Wynn's fly appears to be a hybrid, combining the palmered cock hackle of Halford, the ribbed peacock herl of Foster and the roseate tag of Rolt.

• One feature of the dressed example of the fly contained in the red notebook but not mentioned in the description is that the pink tinsel is continued beneath the hackle to give a single turn at the head. The loops of tinsel on the head were added to simulate the iridescent insect eyes; this was a common feature in JW's wet fly patterns (see later).

• Fished throughout the trout and grayling season. Pattern possibly tied to represent the bumble bee. However, Pennell (1866) suggests that these flies could represent beetles of sorts, the names being colloquially derived thus: beetle … beadle … Mr Bumble (Charles Dickens).

Mike Reed's comments: The pink tinsel was substituted with Uni-Micro Tinsel 6/0, which was a pretty dark pink. This is useful material for tying small tags on any fly and comes in a range of colours.

Naples Yellow Palmer

Taken as a light silverhorn sedge. A very good pattern. Perhaps takes better after a shower of rain which brings down the sedge on the water; can be very useful on such occasions.

HOOK: 14

HACKLE: Naples yellow cock dressed palmer style.

BODY: Light yellow hare's fur.

RIB: Gold wire.

TAG: Luminous orange wool.

Comments

• The brown silverhorn sedge (*Athrissodes cinereus*) is a common sedge fly. They can be seen on most warm summer days, flying very rapidly and strongly in swarms close to the water, usually in the shelter of the banks or overhanging trees or bushes. However, according to Courtney Williams, silverhorns are rarely, if ever, found in trout during autopsies, and may therefore be safely assumed that they are not relished as food. Consequently imitations are of little use to the fly fisherman. However, this does not apply to the hatching pupae, which are eagerly sought by the trout.

• It appears that JW's pattern is dependent on the silverhorn sedge being brought down on the water after rain.

• It is possible that this fly could be used to imitate the yellow sedge (*Psychomia pusilla*). This is the smallest and commonest sedge-fly of any practical value to the fly-fisher. Its distribution is widespread and abundant. Emergence late May to September from early to late evening.

• The length of the anterior wing of the yellow sedge varies between 5mm and 6mm and is a brownish-yellow colour. The antennae are shorter than the wings, fairly stout, and are pale yellowish white with brown annulations.

• The yellow sedge like the silverhorn sedge can sometimes be seen swarming over the middle of the river in the late evening. The females are thought to lay their eggs by dipping on the water.

Mike Reed's comments: Standard tying.

Treacle Parkin

An unorthodox fly, now and
then fairly useful.

HOOK: 15
HACKLE: Ginger cock.
BODY: Peacock herl (green).
TAG: Yellow wool.

Comments

• The Treacle Parkin looks rather like a Coch-y-bondhu with a yellow tail. Those well- known Yorkshire anglers Tim Wilson and Charles Derrick always rated this pattern highly on their home rivers. The Treacle Parkin is also similar to the Red Tag, though the latter has a red tail.

• It is fished both wet and dry, but is probably better as a dry fly than a wet. It is a good trout fly but it is as a grayling fly that it excels.

• Leslie Magee author of *Fly Fishing: The North Country Tradition* (1994) believes that the Treacle Parkin (Yellow Tag) may well be taken for beetles. There are many representations of beetles or 'clocks' in the old North Country lists, this is not surprising because of the large number of terrestrial beetles which are found close to rivers, particularly where they flow through, or are close to woodlands. Beetles find their way to the water surface, especially during the summer and autumn months.

• Norman Roose, former president of the Grayling Society, tied it with a tag of fluorescent arc-chrome wool.

Mike Reed's comments: Standard tying. The green herl is found on the eye feather.

Grey Palmer

For grayling after early frost 'when they
become numb'; I have killed hundreds
of grayling on this fly alone.

HOOK: 14
HACKLE: Badger cock dressed palmer style.
BODY: Black ostrich herl.
RIB: Silver wire.

Comments

• The great value of the palmered hackle on both the wet and floating fly is that it gives the fly an impression of movement and life, and has been termed a 'buzz effect' (John

Roberts, 1995). Scores of different palmers have been developed over the centuries and many still remain today because of their trout-killing qualities. They are used on both rivers and stillwater, and they can be used to represent a hatching or floating sedge, a floating moth, grubs including a caterpillar and, when fished in the surface film in the appropriate colours, a variety of natural hatching duns.

• According to W. Blacker (1843) the Grey Palmer is best fished in April, which possibly ties in with Jim Wynn's comment that the fly is useful after an early morning frost possibly in early April.

• Thomas Best, writing in the *Art of Angling* (1814), recommended the use of suggestive Palmer patterns in the event that an angler does not know what insects or other terrestrials the fish are taking; the Palmer should only be changed when the angler becomes aware of what specific flies the fish are taking.

Mike Reed's comments: Standard tying.

Red Palmer

Probably taken for beetles which fall on the water; now and then will do great execution. Grayling are very fond of it.

HOOK: **14**
HACKLE: **Red cock tied palmer style.**
BODY: **Peacock herl.**
RIB: **Gold wire.**

Comments

• A very old pattern, similar to the lake fly, the Soldier Palmer. Can be fished dry or wet. However, some consider the fly to be best fished well oiled on the top dropper. Excellent general stillwater pattern.

• They can be used to represent a hatching or floating sedge (probably the case for the Red Palmer), a floating moth, a grub and, when fished in the surface film in the appropriate colours, a variety of natural hatching duns.

• William Pilling of Pool Mill (1796) in his list of artificial flies for the River Wharfe recommended using the Red Palmer on warm evenings in June.

Mike Reed's comments: Standard tying.

Mayfly

Where the Mayfly appears this pattern will kill fish at every cast. One of my own private dressings of this fly.

HOOK: 10, longshank

HACKLE: Ginger blue
Andalusian saddle hackle
dyed in luminous
yellow dye.

BODY: 200 denier
white nylon.

RIB: Black Lurex tinsel
and varnish with transparent
acetate yellow nail varnish.

TAIL: Three strands of cock
pheasant fibres.

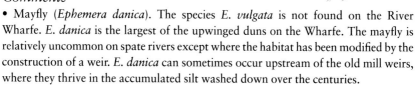

Comments

• Mayfly (*Ephemera danica*). The species *E. vulgata* is not found on the River Wharfe. *E. danica* is the largest of the upwinged duns on the Wharfe. The mayfly is relatively uncommon on spate rivers except where the habitat has been modified by the construction of a weir. *E. danica* can sometimes occur upstream of the old mill weirs, where they thrive in the accumulated silt washed down over the centuries.

• The female dun has grey wings with a blue-green tinge and heavy black veins. They are tinged with yellow along the leading edge. The abdomen is yellow-cream with brownish markings. The legs are creamy-olive and the three tails are dark grey. The male dun has grey wings tinged with yellow and heavy brown veins. The abdomen is greyish-white with brown markings. The legs are dark brown and the three tails are dark grey.

• The duns and spinners can be seen from May until the end of July. The duns usually appear in the afternoons.

Mike Reed's comments: The hackle colour was a challenge! I took a dozen or so ginger cock hackles and used gold wire to tie them in a bunch. Then I prepared a pan of light blue dun dye; once hand hot, I dipped the hackles in, and the wire made a useful handle. Waiting until my fingers got too warm, I removed the hackles and wiped them with kitchen paper. I did this two or three times until the dye took hold but not so much that it would obliterate the ginger. I repeated the process with a yellow dye. This was not as difficult as it might sound. The trick is to wipe the hackles dry after each dip. The black lurex body was again varnished black silk. The yellow varnish was a mix of Veniard's Yellow and Clear varnish. For the floss body, I used Uni-Glo floss, 600 denier phosphorescent white.

Mayfly Half-Spent

Very useful. Was at one time a favourite on Chelker Reservoir, where a 'battered' fly was often preferred.

HOOK: 10, longshank.

HACKLE: Grey mallard dyed in luminous yellow dye.

FRONT HACKLE: White cock dyed greenish yellow.

BODY: 200 denier yellowish green nylon.

TAIL: Bronze mallard fibres.

Comments

• The example of dyed cock hackle provided by JW had a short fibre brown badger-like centre to the hackle. This is probably to aid the buoyancy of the fly.

• Mayfly (*Ephemera danica*). Useful in the evening, when the female mayfly return from the surrounding vegetation where they had mated; they dip onto the water to lay their eggs before lying spent on the surface. Sometimes the trout begin to rise, taking the spent fly in preference to all others.

Mike Reed's comments: Use Veniard Yellow Fluoro dye for the hackle and a mix of yellow and olive dye for the body material which is Uni-Glo floss, 600 denier phosphorescent white. One of the nicest Mayfly patterns I have tied.

Fisherman's Curse

Taken on reservoirs when spent fly falls on the water; must be made even smaller for the river.

HOOK: 16

HACKLE: Whitish cream cock.

BODY: White nylon.

THORAX: Cock pheasant tail herl.

TAIL: Three fibres white cock.

Comments

• Fisherman's curse, angler's curse or white curse (*Caenis* and *Brachycercus spp*). Aptly nicknamed as the tiny duns treat your person as an ideal place on which to carry out their amazing quick change into spinners, and land in their hundreds on face, hands clothing and everywhere they can. If you have your polarised sunglasses on, they have the nasty habit of crawling inside and outside of the lenses, and can obscure vision by 50 per cent or more.

• The family has six distinct species: *Brachycercus harrisella*, *Caenis horaria*, *C. robusta*, *C. rivulorum*, *C. luctosa* and *C. macrura*. They are all so similar that only an experienced entomologist can separate them.

• Feeding trout will often start taking the emerging nymphs, change to the hatching dun and within a short time change again to the returning spent spinners. The total adult life-span is less than 90 minutes, and consequently, the fly-fisher never quite knows on which stage individual trout are feeding. We suggest that the very start of the hatch is your only real chance of tempting a fish with a *Caenis* imitation. May be the best place to be during a *Caenis* hatch is somewhere else!

• *Caenis* usually hatch in the early evening, particularly in conditions of a calm or gentle breeze in the summer months.

Mike Reed's comments: Standard tying. The white body material is strands of Uni-Glo floss, 600 denier phosphorescent white.

Orange Tag

Invented some 150 years ago by a Wharfedale angler for use on the Wharfe at Ilkley. I know one angler who uses nothing else.

HOOK: 15

HACKLE: Red cock.

BODY: Peacock herl (green).

TAG: Orange wool.

Comments

• This is a variant of the Red Tag with an orange tail comprising orange wool, floss or fibres of an orange feather. A common name for this fly in Yorkshire is the 'Treacle Parkin'.

• Very useful grayling fly, but also a successful trout fly. It can be fished both dry and wet. This fly is also thought to be an imitation of a beetle.

Mike Reed's comments: Standard tying. Again use the Veniard wool for any tag/tail.

Hackled Red Spinner Dry Fly

HOOK: 14

THORAX: Green peacock herl.

HACKLE: Light blue
Andalusian cock hackle.

BODY: Detached.
Place needle in vice as per
McClelland's (1949) idea
for detached bodies. Lay along
needle three strands of human hair
or rabbit whiskers together with a
length of orange tinsel, over which,
wind a length of strip cellophane dyed
darkish red, about one eighth of an inch in width, previously soaked in luke-warm
water. Wind towards you, then rib with orange tinsel, giving the whole a coating of
transparent Celline varnish. Allow time to dry then slide off the needle and transfer
to hook, tying in the surplus firmly. Form a thorax of green peacock herl, over which,
wind a light blue Andalusian cock hackle. Allow half width of cellophane for overlap
in making body.

Comments

• Published in the *Fishing Gazette* (1943) but did not appear in JW's notebook of dry
fly dressings.

• This pattern may represent several species including:

Autumn spinner (*Ecdyonurus dispar*). Habitat – stony rivers and stony shores of lakes.
Emergence – early evening from July to early October. It is seldom seen on the water
in quantity. The body of the male spinner is bright red/brown, with transparent wings
and heavy brown veining, long, dark brown tails and brownish legs.

Large brook spinner (*Ecdyonurus torrentis*). Habitat – stony streams and rivers.
Hatches are sparse and occur during the day and early evening from late March to
July. The female is often referred to as the large red spinner. They have transparent
wings with dark-brown to black veining and yellowish leading edges. Their bodies are
dark olive brown, banded with red to purple-brown, their venters are purple.

Large dark olive spinner (*Baetis rhodani*). Habitat – stony streams and rivers. This
species is not common on Northern rivers.

Medium olive spinner (*Baetis vernus*, *B. tenax* and *B. buceratus*). Habitat – streams
and rivers. Both (*B. vernus* and *B. tenax*) are widespread in England and Scotland.
They emerge during the day or early evening throughout the summer with a peak in
May and June. Hatches are often heavy. This species is largely responsible for the
season's first serious evening rises towards the middle of May. Swarms of male spinners

form in the early evenings over the river banks and the females crawl underwater on weed-stems to lay their eggs. The spinners die, float to the surface and then drift downstream just below the surface film.

Small dark olive spinner (*Baetis scambus*). Habitat – streams and rivers. Hatches mid-day to late evening from June until November; with a peak in July and August. The female is referred to as the small red spinner. The males usually swarm over the banks or in the shelter of adjacent trees or bushes. The females crawl underwater to lay their eggs and eventually die. Spent and dying spinners are swept down stream and then up to the surface where they drift down beneath the surface film. The chosen artificial should be fished like-wise.

Mike Reed's comments: This was a bit of a one off, not too sure why Jim Wynn included it! Follow the instructions carefully.

Part Two

*Background and context to
fly-fishing in Wharfedale:
natural history and geology,
the North Country Style
and notable fly-fishermen*

William Brumfitt (1846–1926)

River Wharfe catchment area

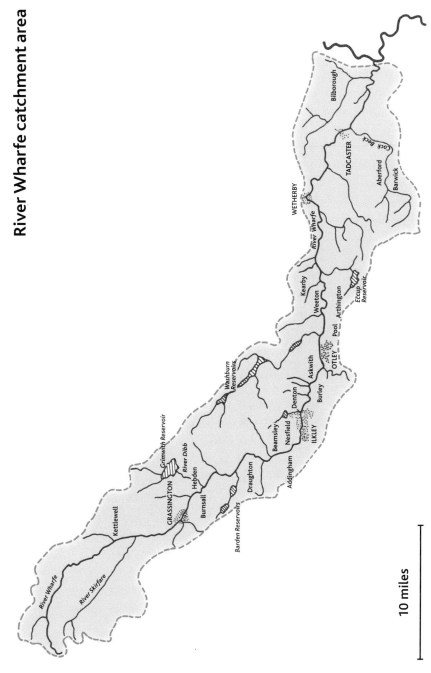

10 miles

1 The course of the River Wharfe, its landscape and geology

The River Wharfe is a river located in Yorkshire, England. From its source to its confluence with the River Ouse, the River Wharfe is approximately 97km (60 miles) in length. Steeped in angling history the River Wharfe carves its way through the heart of the Yorkshire Dales, providing some of the best trout and grayling habitat in Northern England. For much of its length it is the county boundary between West Yorkshire and North Yorkshire.

The Roman document known as the *Notitia Dignitatum (etiam vide infra)* provides details of the disposition of the Roman army as it was in the 4th–5th Centuries, listing the civil and military posts and the location of every military command of the Duke of the Britains between Danvm (Doncaster) and Arbeia (South Shields). This publication also gave the origin of the name of the River Wharfe, which apparently stems from an original Celtic river-name meaning 'the winding one'; perhaps relating to Old Scandinavian *hvarf* or *hverfi* meaning 'a bend or corner'. It is also interesting to note that on an Ilkley Roman altar stone (vide RIB 635 infra) is a reference to a local female Roman deity Verbeia, The Goddess of the River Wharfe.

Running from north to south, Wharfedale is one of the Yorkshire Dales' longest and most beautiful valleys. As a matter of convention, Wharfedale is often divided into what is arbitrarily known as Upper Wharfedale, Mid Wharfedale and Lower Wharfedale. Upper Wharfedale lies upstream of the villages of Grassington and Threshfield. Mid Wharfedale is below Grassington as far as Linton, and Lower Wharfedale downstream of Linton. Tributary valleys of Upper Wharfedale include Langstrothdale and Littondale, whilst tributary valleys of Mid Wharfedale include Dibbledale, Skyredale, the Valley of Desolation, Kexdale and Washburn Valley.

Upper Wharfedale

Landscape and geology

The characteristic landscape of Upper Wharfedale and Littondale is the result of a subtle combination of physical processes and and also by the influence of people. The salient physical influences on the landscape have been the nature of the underlying geology, the effect of glacial and interglacial periods and the resultant thin, immature soils reflected in the nature of vegetation and agricultural practices in the dale.

In parts of Upper Wharfedale the valley is broad and has an overall smooth shape. This form resulted from the various glacial periods, the last of which reached its peak 20,000 years ago during which time both the dales and fells were covered in ice. As the climate became warmer, about 15,000 years ago, the melting of the valley glacier resulted in the formation of a number of retreat moraines, such as those across the valley at Skirfare Bridge, Mill Scar Lash and Drebley, each of which resulted in the temporary formation of a glacial lake in the valley, contributing to the very flat floor in parts of Upper Wharfedale. Where glacial lakes formed, some overflowed and cut hanging valleys and channels in the valley sides, creating complex features, such as those above Storiths, near Bolton Abbey. At Conistone, a meltwater channel created a waterfall which retreated back into the hillside creating Dib Scar, and below it, the limestone gorge Conistone Dib, both now dry features as the water flows underground. Since the end of the Ice Age the erosive action of the River Wharfe and its tributaries has created water falls, narrow gorges, river

The confluence of the River Wharfe and the River Skirfare

cliffs and deposited patches of sand and shingle along the river sides. A series of terraces and levees can be seen on the valley sides of Wharfedale. These represent periods of major fluvial erosion and post glacial deposition.

The geology of Upper Wharfedale is complex, but essentially comprises layers of rocks, mainly types of limestone, which have been exposed through the effects of glaciation, natural weathering, hydrological effects and the influence of the Mid Craven and North Craven fault lines and localised up-thrusting of rocks such as the Skyreholme folds. The two main types of limestone are the Great Scar Limestone, a pure limestone about 180m thick, and the overlying rock which comprises a series of four or five thin bands of limestone intermixed with thin shales and occasional sandstones, known as the Yoredale Beds. Both types of rock exert characteristic influences over the landscape. The Great Scar Limestone is a lighter coloured almost white rock, outcropping to form dramatic cliffs such as those at Kilnsey Crag (a spur of land truncated by the effects of glaciation) and, less prominent, at Grass Wood. The Yoredale Beds are slightly darker in appearance and exert the greatest influence on valley form, outcropping for miles along Upper Wharfedale north of Kettlewell, along each side of Littondale and along Langstrothdale, creating a very characteristic stepped or terraced appearance.

In addition to the cliffs and scars which are a prominent feature of the valley, Upper Wharfedale exhibits many other features associated with classic karstic scenery. These include gorges, as at Conistone, dry valleys, shake holes, sink holes, swallow holes and springs, together with caves and areas of glacial karst limestone pavement, such as the pavement above Conistone.

In addition to the above-ground landscape, an underground landscape of passages, caves, pools and streams, waterfalls, stalactites and stalagmites has developed as a result of dissolution by water percolating through the limestone. This underground scenery is best represented at caves such as Dow Cave near Kettlewell and Boreham Cave in Littondale. Boulders carried by the ice, have been left strewn on the hillsides and in the valley bottom. Some of the boulders are of a different rock type than those in the local area (hence known as erratics). Pieces of non-local stone carried by the ice can often be found within dry stone walls.

In Upper Wharfedale the soils that have developed on the upper valley sides are peaty and acidic, and fairly infertile, supporting a limited range of plant species including heather, cotton grass, bilberry and bracken and plantations of coniferous trees. On the valley floor and lower valley sides, soils formed by the effects of fluvial and glacial deposition are richer and support rich pasture

The River Wharfe at Kilnsey

land grazed by cattle and sheep. The soils on the margins of the pastures have allowed the development of mixed broadleaved woodland.

It is important to appreciate that the characteristic landscape of Upper Wharfedale which is largely controlled by the geology has resulted in a river which has a unique character. The characteristics of the River Wharfe in Upper Wharfedale are described briefly in the following sections.

Oughtershaw to Buckden

The source of the River Wharfe is Oughtershaw Beck in the Yorkshire Dales National Park, which flows between Outershaw Side on the flank of Dodd Fell to the north and Oughtershaw Moss on the flanks of Cocklee Fell to the south (source elevation approximately 380m). Oughtershaw Beck becomes the River Wharfe south of Oughtershaw. A tributary stream, Greenfield Beck joins the Wharfe from the east at Beckermonds in Langstrothdale Chase. From Langstrothdale the Wharfe flows southeast within a narrow steep-sided valley founded on limestone, through the hamlets of Beckermonds, Yockenthwaite and Hubberholme. Hubberholme is famous for its church, the resting place of the writer J.B. Priestley. The George public house in Hubberholme also has some sizeable stuffed brown trout specimens captured from the River Wharfe during low water in pools between Yokenthwaite and Buckden. At

Buckden at the head of Upper Wharfedale the valley opens out and becomes flat bottomed, with level fields between which the river meanders. Cray Beck enters the Wharfe near Buckden. The White Lion in Cray is also well worth a visit.

Buckden to Grassington

From Buckden its southwards course in Upper Wharfedale flows through the villages of Starbotton, Kettlewell, near Conistone, and Kilnsey. Above Kilnsey the valley is wide and level, being a former lake bed. At Kilnsey is the famous Kilnsey Crag, a dramatic overhanging limestone cliff, popular with climbers and tourists. There is also a good rainbow trout fishery adjacent to the Tennants Arms public house in Kilnsey. Between Kettlewell and Kilnsey at Amerdale Dub the River Wharfe is joined by the tributary valley of Littondale and the River Skirfare. The River Skirfare rises on the moors below the eastern flank of Pen-y-Ghent and passes the hamlets of Foxup and Halton Gill and the villages of Litton and Arncliffe. The Skirfare, after its constituent becks have dashed down from the fells, also has a slower passage before it joins the River Wharfe. The Kilnsey Angling Club has a very nice fishing hut at the Skirfare/Wharfe confluence at Amerdale Dub. The upper Wharfe has a catchment which includes both Carboniferous Limestone and glacial deposits and the riverbed is variously formed on limestone bedrock, loose gravels, cobbles, silt and clay. The flow varies from shallow riffles in the gravel sections to slow-running deep pools over silt. Downstream from Kilnsey the River Wharfe runs in a narrow valley and passes between the villages of Grassington and Threshfield.

Mosses that are characteristic of upland rivers are found on the limestone rocks, including *Cincliotus fontinaloides*, *Rhyncostegium riparioides* and *Chiloscyphus polyanthes*. On the banks are occasional stands of common reed and reed canary-grass. Willow scrub favours overgrown tributary streams and is accompanied by a variety of sedges, for example, bottle sedge, slender tufted-sedge and lesser pond sedge, while the nationally rare northern spike rush is found in wet hollows and meanders. In the riverside meadows between Buckden and Kettlewell there are stands of a species-poor sedge community, dominated by one or two sedge species, usually the tall lesser pond sedge or bottle sedge. The contrasting upland/lowland nature of the upper river is reflected in the birdlife, with both dipper and kingfisher present.

The Skirfare and the upper reaches of the Wharfe are very similar in nature, where, due to the speed of the current fewer aquatic plant and faunal species can exist. Here the river and its feeder streams have a plentiful supply of oxygen due to their numerous waterfalls and rapids, but the speed of the current prevents sediments forming on the bed of the river. Creatures living here such as nymphs of ephemeroptera and stoneflies are specialists at 'hanging on' and have streamlined bodies to enable them to do so. Caddis flies living here commonly do not live in cases but spin webs and have large hooks on their rear to enable them to hang on. The upper Wharfe is important for its population of native white-clawed crayfish which are under threat from 'crayfish plague,' carried by the North American signal crayfish, a larger and more aggressive species, which is also found in the Wharfe. The signal crayfish have colonised the river near Kilnsey and above Grassington, but good populations of the native species remain at Kilnsey, Grassington, Burnsall and Appletreewick. Fine lined pea mussel is also to be found.

Mid Wharfedale

Landscape and geology

The Mid and North Craven Fault cross the dale in an east to west direction between Grassington and Burnsall. The underlying rock changes abruptly from mostly limestones to the north to thick layers of shales to the south off the Mid Craven Fault. A complex undulating topography and vegetation changes occur across the fault lines. To the south of the Mid Craven Fault is a line of green dome-shaped hills known as the Cracoe Reef Knolls (the two Kail Hills, Stebden and Elbolton). The reef knolls comprise conical mounds of pure limestone which 330 million years ago formed part of a seabed reef and were eventually buried in mud, which has since eroded, leaving the knolls exposed as features within the valley floor and on the valley sides. These features represent the national classic example of their type.

Skyredale, a tributary valley of the northern part of Mid Wharfedale is of particular geological interest as it marks the approximate boundary of the Skyreholme Anticline and the South Craven Fault. The Skyreholme Anticline has thrust limestone to the surface and is visible as darker coloured limestone at Loup Scar and Trollers Gill. The Skyreholme anticline pushed up the mineral veins which resulted in the past development of ore fields at Grassington Moor, Greenhow Hill, Appletreewick and the fells above Conistone and Buckden.

The underlying geology of Mid Wharfedale comprises mainly sandstones and shales of the Millstone Grit Series, which extend over the majority of the valley floor and on moor tops at Barden Fell and Barden Moor. The rock comprises of a coarse-grained, yellow-brown sandstone, which is seen outcropping as sandstone free faces on the moor tops, for example at Simons Seat and Earls Seat. Bowland Shales can be seen outcropping by the river at Bolton Abbey and near Bolton Bridge. Complexity is added by the Skipton Anticline that has thrust underlying limestone to the surface, visible above and below the Cavendish Pavilion, upstream of Bolton Abbey.

The Millstone Grit outcrops at the well known Cow and Calf Rocks at Ilkley and forms a rolling dissected plateau to the south. The moorland areas above Ilkley have developed on the Millstone Grit rocks. These moorland areas comprise blanket bogs and mires and in drier areas have wet and dry heaths and acid grasslands.

In Mid Wharfedale around Otley the coarse sandstones are known as the Yeadon, Guiseley and Bramhope Grits. The Otley Shell Beds have been exposed in the huge landslide complexes which cover Otley Chevin to the south. The Otley Shell Beds is one of the youngest horizons to yield trilobites at surface exposures in Britain. It is rich in the remains of many of the animals that inhabited the Carboniferous Sea. Glacial lakes filled Mid Wharfedale at one time and deposited large valley trains of sand and gravel, which have been quarried at Ben Rhydding, Otley and Knotford Knook. Remains of mammoth, woolly rhinoceros and elk have been found in the gravel deposits.

The River Wharfe at Barden Bridge

Grassington to Bolton Abbey

Below Grassington and Threshfield the valley is known as Mid Wharfedale and the river flows through the settlements of Linton, Hebden, Burnsall and Appletreewick. The River Dibb within Dibbledale flows out of Grimwith Reservoir and under Dibble's Bridge before joining the River Wharfe between Burnsall and Appletreewick. The River Dibb is one of England's shortest rivers. Blands Beck is a tributary stream of the River Wharfe which enters the Wharfe just below Appletreewick. Skyredale is the valley of Blands Beck, which runs by the hamlets of Skyreholme and Upper Skyreholme beneath the gritstone edge of Simon's Seat.

The Wharfe has a reputation of being very dangerous, in that many people have drowned while crossing, swimming or fishing in it. Slightly north of Bolton Abbey is The Strid, a point at which the whole river is channeled through a narrow gorge. At its narrowest, it is less than two metres across at the surface. The gap looks eminently jumpable but this is deceptive due to the fact that many of the ledges on the sides are at different levels and are often very slippery. Scottish throne hopeful, 'The Boy from Egremont', immortalised

The River Wharfe at Barden Aqueduct

in the Orkeyinga and in a poem by William Wordsworth; drowned here in 1157 while attempting to leap across the gap on horseback. Barry and Lyn Collett, a couple on their honeymoon drowned here in August 1998 and their bodies were not recovered for several weeks. Fierce currents that run through this section drag down any hapless victim, where they become trapped among the underwater ledges and hollows carved by the rapids. Bolton Abbey and Bolton Woods are extremely popular in the summer months. The ruins and chapel of Bolton Abbey, river pasture and beautiful Strid Woods are the main attractions along this particularly lovely stretch of the River Wharfe. This section of the River Wharfe has a very rich fly-fishing history.

Bolton Abbey to Otley

South of Bolton Abbey the River Wharfe passes out of the Yorkshire Dales National Park. Posforth Gill which flows within the Valley of Desolation is a tributary stream which enters the River Wharfe just east of Bolton Abbey. Kexdale and the tributary stream of Kex Beck flow into the River Wharfe near the hamlet of Beamsley. Goosanders are present along the Wharfe from Strid Woods to Burley-in-Wharfedale. The dipper, kingfisher and grey wagtail can be seen throughout the Wharfedale valley. Below Bolton Abbey the current is slower and is enriched by farm manure and the treated waste from sewage works at villages upstream. Sediments are deposited enabling both aquatic and marginal plants to become established. These in turn become habitats for different species of caddis flies, crustaceans, and beetle larvae. *Ephemeroptera* and midge larvae thrive in such conditions.

Downstream of Bolton Abbey the Wharfe flows through the settlements of Beamsley, Addingham and Ilkley. Below Ilkley the river broadens and levels out, constricted only by the bridging-point at Otley. A significant tributary stream, Bow Beck enters the Wharfe at Ben Rhydding. Between Burley in Wharfedale and Otley, the course of the River Wharfe was diverted and straightened to allow the construction of a new section of the A65(T).

The stretch between Otley and Pool includes several good runs and pools including the Otley Weir pools, the Mill Pool, White Bridge run and the Sand Banks below Farnley Hall estate.

There are records of water voles, from Grassington and Otley, but unfortunately there have been no recent sightings. There is, however, a healthy population of water voles at Netherby. Otters use the River Wharfe in certain areas, and some artificial holts have been built to encourage them to stay. Mink are present throughout Wharfedale.

Washburn Valley

South of Otley the tributary valley of the River Washburn enters the River Wharfe upstream of Pool near Leathley. The Cayton Gill Beds extend north from the Washburn valley to Masham. These strata comprise muddy sandstones and siltstones which contain many remains of brachiopods and bivalves. Armscliff Crag overlooks both the Washburn and Wharfe valleys, and is one of the largest and most massive gritstone tors in the region. The isolated crag comprises competent rock that is less jointed then the surrounding material which has been weathered or eroded away. The River Washburn has been dammed to form Thruscross, Fewston, Swinsty and Lindley Wood Reservoirs which supply drinking water to Leeds. Much of the catchment area of the Washburn is covered with conifer plantations. The Fewston and Swinsty reservoirs are popular rainbow trout fisheries. The Washburn valley is a rich birding area. Heron, grey wagtail and dipper may be found. The alder/oak/birch woodland along the banks of the River Washburn provides a habitat for tits, mistle and song thrush, tree creeper, wren, great spotted woodpecker, tawny owl, woodcock, sparrow hawk, gold crest, bull finch and lesser spotted wood pecker. In the summer you can expect to see spotted and pied fly catchers, common red start, willow warbler, chiff chaff, black cap, garden warbler, gold finch and occasionally wood warbler. The string of reservoirs can produce a variety of wildfowl, including, great crested grebe, heron, mallard, tufted duck, Canada and graylag geese, moorhen and osprey. During the winter goldeneye, pochard, goosander and teal can be seen. Waders use the mud at Lindley Wood reservoir in late summer when the water level has fallen. The Washburn valley is also important for liverworts and mosses which are sufficiently rare to have their own Biodiversity Action Plans. Violet crystalwort is found at Fewston and Swinsty reservoirs and dwarf bladder moss can be found at Lindley Wood reservoir.

Pool in Wharfedale to Linton

Downstream of Otley the River Wharfe flows at a leisurely pace through the settlements of Pool, Castley, Netherby, Chapel Hill, Collingham, Linton, Wetherby, Boston Spa, Thorpe Arch, Newton Kyme and Tadcaster. Between Pool and Collingham the River Wharfe meanders in wide arcs across the broad valley. Between Pool and Otley the northern valley side comprises arable farmland belonging to Farnley Hall. Several important tributary streams enter the Wharfe between Pool-in-Wharfedale and Collingham these include Riffa Beck and Weeton Beck. A high embankment and 21 arch railway viaduct

The Wharfe at Harewood Bridge

spans the River Wharfe at Arthington. The broad valley floor around Castley and Arthington comprises rich pasture land. The A61(T) crosses the river at Harewood Bridge. The dramatic ruins of Harewood Castle can be seen on the top of the southern valley side. An ancient ford crosses the River Wharfe between Harewood and Netherby. There are a number of accounts of people being drowned at this ford when the river has been in flood. A large tributary stream, Collingham Beck, draining land to the south of Collingham, joins the Wharfe near Linton. The Collingham Beck swells very quickly during heavy rain and often floods the centre of Collingham. The River Wharfe is noted to be dangerous at Collingham, with undercurrents especially prevalent around Linton Road bridge and the former viaduct.

Lower Wharfedale

Landscape and geology

Downstream of Linton and Wetherby the landscape changes. This is largely due to the change in the underlying geology, where the younger Permian strata of the Lower Magnesian Limestone Formation rest unconformably on the older Carboniferous strata. The Lower Magnesian Limestone dip gently to the east and is characterised by a softer more friable limestone with a yellowish or reddish brown colouration. The River Wharfe has cut through the Lower Magnesian Limestone creating steep sided river gorges and river cliffs. The narrow parts of the valley between Wetherby and Boston Spa are wooded.

The Lower Magnesian Limestone is an important building stone and has been used to construct buildings not only in the local area but in other areas of Yorkshire including York Minster. The Lower Magnesian Limestone geology gives rise to a gently rolling landscape characterized by productive, intensively farmed agricultural land. The light soils on top of the Magnesian Limestone proved attractive for early farmers as opposed to the heavier clay soils of the Vale of York. The fields are often large, bounded by low cut hawthorn hedges, creating a generally open landscape where the valley is broad.

During the last glacial period the River Wharfe was blocked by ice located in the Vale of York. Consequently, the original course of the River Wharfe which flowed from Wetherby towards the north east was diverted towards the south east to cut the winding gorge which now runs alongside the village of Thorpe Arch.

Linton to Tadcaster

South of Linton between Wetherby, Newton Kyme and Boston Spa the river runs through rich pasture and arable farmland. A large bridge and weir crosses the river at Wetherby. The weir pool at Wetherby contains some good size barbel. Boston Spa was a famous Spa town on the River Wharfe; the pump room and baths are located just upstream of Boston towards Newton Kyme where sulphur springs are present. The River Wharfe between Boston Spa and Newton Kyme is relatively wide and there are some very deep pools. The river passes through a deep gorge near Boston Spa Bridge. There is a weir present just below the bridge. This holds good size trout, grayling and barbel. In recent years pike over 25lb have been taken from this section of river. An eleven arch viaduct crosses the River Wharfe approximately a quarter of a mile north of Tadcaster. This used to be part of the Leeds to York Railway authorized in 1846, which ceased operation in 1955. The viaduct carried a siding that serviced a mill on the east side of the River Wharfe.

In the section between Tadcaster and Bramham the River Wharfe is a wide river and in places has cut steep river cliffs in the Cadeby Formation of the Lower Magnesian Limestone. The groundwater within the Magnesian Limestone aquifer is an important source of water for the breweries located in Tadcaster. The groundwater is rich in lime sulphate and when groundwater

The Wharfe at Tadcaster

levels are high, freshwater springs, known locally as 'popple-wells', can be seen issuing out of the ground near St Mary's Church, Tadcaster. Upstream of the road bridge in Tadcaster was the site of the ancient ford which was used to cross the river. Tadcaster was founded by the Romans, who named it Calcaria from the Latin word for lime, reflecting the importance of the area's limestone geology as a natural resource for quarrying, an industry which continues today. The Roman settlement of Calcaria was constructed adjacent to the ford. Calcaria was an important staging post on the road to Eburacum (York), which grew up at the river crossing. In the 11th Century William de Percy established Tadcaster Castle, a motte-and-bailey fortress, near the present town centre using stone reclaimed from Roman remains. The castle was abandoned in the early 12th Century, and though briefly re-fortified with cannon emplacements during the Civil War, all that remains is the castle motte. The original crossing was probably a simple ford near the present site of St Mary's Church, soon followed by a wooden bridge. Around 1240, the first stone bridge was constructed close by. The current road bridge was constructed in the early part of the 18th Century and was constructed from stone from the remains of the former bridge and castle. Tax registers from 1314 record the presence of two thriving breweries or brewhouses in the town, one paying 8d in tax and the other 4d. Three breweries are still present, The Tower Brewery (Coors, formely Bass), John Smith's and Samuel Smith's Old Brewery, which is the oldest brewery in Yorkshire. The weir pool at Tadcaster has been a popular place for fishing, and some large barbel have been caught in this part of the river.

Tadcaster to Cawood

Below Tadcaster, Lower Wharfedale opens out and becomes part of the Vale of York. The River Wharfe has been and still is a particularly good coarse fishery along this stretch. However, this section of the river during the 1700s was noted for its salmon fishing and large salmon runs. The salmon fishing below Tadcaster belonged to the Fielding's of Grimstone. In the vicinity of Acaster and Cawood are the remains of salmon garths which formerly belonged to the Archbishops of York. The salmon runs diminished during the 1800s due to pollution of the River Ouse, principally caused by the heavily polluted tributary of the River Aire. The river pollution was caused by the industrial cities of Bradford and Leeds.

Two small streams, which drain the higher land between Bilbrough, Healaugh, Wighill and Walton, after a course of three miles, join into one stream called Catterton Beck. Catterton Beck flows southwards for several miles and joins the River Wharfe at the ancient settlement of Bolton Percy, located three miles east of Tadcaster. The River Wharfe flows in a south easterly direction through the settlements of Kirkby Wharfe, Ulleskelf and Ryther. A railway bridge spans the river at Ulleskelf. Two inns in the centre of Ulleskelf were popular for fishermen staying to fish the Wharfe in this area.

Between Ryther and Cawood the Wharfe is very much a lowland river, winding in sweeping curves under overhanging willows. Beyond Ryther the Wharfe then flows into the River Ouse at Wharfe's Mouth about half a mile north of Cawood which stands on the banks of the River Ouse. The River Wharfe is a public navigation from the weir at Tadcaster to its junction with the River Ouse near Cawood. The River Wharfe is tidal from Ulleskelf.

2   Fly-fishing on the River Wharfe and the North Country Style

The upland rivers of northern England tend to be spate rivers which rise quickly following heavy rain. They usually provide rough, streamy and stony water with a series of pools and runs offering a varied challenge to fly-fishermen. The River Wharfe is probably the most famous of the Yorkshire rivers, maybe because of the top quality fly-fishing it provides, or perhaps because it is set within some of the Yorkshire Dales' most outstanding scenery. The Wharfe can rise very quickly after heavy rainfall higher up in the dale. Often some of the best fly fishing is provided when the river is fining down after rainfall.

The Wharfe is a similar size to the River Ure and like all the Yorkshire Dales rivers it runs with a peat stain, giving it the appearance of a pint of Yorkshire bitter. Fly-fishing is top class with good stocks of wild brown trout and also grayling. Access to good fly-fishing on the River Wharfe is much better than the River Ure and there are many miles of good and varied fly-fishing water. The River Wharfe along its length provides a series of runs, pools and glides and therefore offers a multitude of different types of water. The different types of water demand many different fly fishing skills and methods. No two days are the same when fishing the River Wharfe.

Care must be taken when wading as there are many hazards, including strong currents, deep shelves, slippery rocks, boulder strewn beds; a wading staff can be useful in places. It is said that the Wharfe is one of the fastest rising spate rivers in Europe, so extra care should be taken when wading during rainy periods.

The rich waters of the River Wharfe attract many kinds of flora and fauna and a day spent fly-fishing usually results in the sighting of dippers, kingfishers and grey and pied wagtails in or near the water. Away from the water we can see curlews, lapwings, kestrels, buzzards, hares, stoats and weasels. The Wharfe together with other Yorkshire rivers shares the same characteristics in that they are all different and all need to be understood; their moods, their fish and hidden corners.

Introducing the North Country Style

Fly-fishing on the River Wharfe started a long time ago and is steeped with tradition for its wet fly fishing, or the North Country Style fishing as it is known. The writings of past North Country Style masters such as Pilling, Swarbrick, Brumfitt, Lister, Pritt, Edmonds and Lee, and Walbran take their place in angling lore and history. The typical approach on the River Wharfe has always been to fish suggestive rather than purely imitative flies, dressed to imitate a variety of food forms, including nymphs and adult flies. The fish in this fast flowing freestone environment often have only a split second to make up their mind whether the fly presented to them represents a natural food source or not. For this reason the soft-hackled wet fly patterns are an ideal fly to use as they are designed to be suggestive patterns.

It should be remembered that on a riffle most of the trout's food is taken beneath the surface. A large proportion of nymphs as they rise to the surface before hatching are carried downstream before they reach the surface. Many of the emerging insects do not succeed to break free of the nymphal shuck or do emerge but are drowned before they reach the surface. Some insect species are adapted to live within or just below the surface of the water. Many other adult flies, including terrestrials which have fallen into the turbulent water, become water logged. Species such as the *Baetis* mayfly spinners lay their eggs below the surface of the water and are carried by the current in the process. The North Country fly patterns are designed to imitate these different insect forms which are readily accepted as food by trout and grayling. The soft hackle was designed to be mobile and to undulate in the current, thereby suggesting the movements of water-borne insects and/or other water fauna. These patterns were invented for the Yorkshire Dales rivers and other northern, fast flowing, rain-fed rivers, using simple, locally available materials.

Traditionally the North Country Style method entailed using a relatively long rod and casting a short length of line. For this to be successful it was important to watch the fly line and to keep in touch with the fly by raising the rod tip and sometimes retrieving line with the other hand. When a fish takes, there is often no more sign than the slight straightening of the line, but now and then there is an obvious splash as a trout or grayling takes the fly. The North Country patterns can be cast across and slightly downstream, or they may be cast upstream and/or upstream and across, carefully negotiating skinny riffles and likely looking runs. These two wet fly-fishing methods are discussed in further detail later in the chapter.

Many of the North Country patterns are a great way of searching water quickly and when the fish are near the surface they are devastating. Fishing the North Country wet flies is a very enjoyable and relaxing way to fly-fish, however, it also requires a high level of fly-fishing skill to fish effectively.

Origins of the North Country Style

Although William Pilling of Pool-in-Wharfedale produced a list of flies for the River Wharfe in 1794, the onset of the North Country Style would appear to be based on the distinctive patterns found in a manuscript written by John Swarbrick. The original list of John Swarbrick's fly patterns was dated 1807, however, the list was not published until 1907 as a *List of Wharfedale Flies*. This publication also included additional flies added by J. W. Sagar of Ilkley, dating from about 1890. E. Beanlands published a small pamphlet containing the lists of Swarbrick's and Sagar's flies. Swarbrick's list of flies was modified and refined by later generations of northern anglers including Pickard, Turton, Theakston, Jackson, Brumfitt and Lister.

It was not until 78 years after Swarbrick that two important pieces of work detailing the tying and the methods of fishing North Country fly patterns were published. Firstly, T. E. Pritt's book *Yorkshire Trout Flies* in 1885 became the reference for fishing North Country patterns. Edmonds and Lee then published their book *Brook and River Trouting* in 1916. Both books were important pieces of work that drew on their own experiences and also those of other anglers and importantly the river keepers of the River Wharfe. The river keepers on the famed Bolton Abbey section of the River Wharfe and the Appletreewick, Barden and Burnsall water have always played a huge part in the River Wharfe's fly-fishing history. Sylvester Lister was not only the founder member of the Burnsall Angling Club in 1873 but was also the river keeper, and was regarded as both an expert fly-tyer and fisher. Pritt, Edmonds and Lee and other angling authors such as Max Walbran were largely responsible for copying, collating and refining existing North Country fly patterns at the turn of the 19th Century.

T. E. Pritt was a very important spokesperson for the North Country Style. Pritt clearly understood the value of the nymph at a time when many fishermen were ignorant of its value. By 1860 the North Country School fishermen had largely abandoned the winged wet fly patterns in favour of the sparsely dressed soft-hackled patterns. Pritt along with his predecessors of the North Country Style had recognised that trout find it easy to take still-born duns which have been crunched around in the turbulent conditions of spate rivers, and they had the courage to break away from the mainstream and design radical new dressings to take advantage of their theories.

As long ago as 1886, Pritt said: 'It is now conceded that a fly dressed hackle-wise is generally to be preferred to a winged imitation. The reasons for this are not far to seek, and are satisfactory. It is far more difficult to imitate a perfect insect and to afterwards impart to it a semblance of life in or on the water, than it is to produce something which is sufficiently near a resemblance of an imperfectly developed insect, struggling to attain the surface of the stream. Trout undoubtedly take a hackled fly for the insect just rising from the pupa in a half-drowned state; and the opening and closing of the fibres or feathers give it an appearance of vitality, which, even the most dexterous fly-fisher will fail to impart to the winged imitation.'

Pritt was one of the first anglers to question the fundamental premise of the design of the wet fly; pointing out the inconsistencies in the design and theory of its use, particularly on North Country rivers. His two best known books, *The Book of the Grayling* and *North Country Flies*, guaranteed him a place in fly-fishing's hall of fame. His death at the young age of 47 from influenza was as unexpected as it was tragic.

In the years leading up to the turn of the century, a stand-off developed between the northern English and Scottish anglers on one side and the southern chalk stream fishermen on the other. The failure of each side to grasp the problems posed by river conditions which the other faced, led to decades of argument. Many books of the era included a section in which a group of northern (or southern) visiting fly-fishermen were trounced by the application of the 'proper' technique. It is unfortunate that there was little cross-fertilization and adaptation of both techniques. North Country Style fly-fishing works perfectly well outside its accepted northern range. The reason may well be that by the time the North Country Style was properly established, no southern angler in his right mind would have tried it; the penalty for such heresy was rejection and exclusion by his incensed fellow club members. Northern anglers did use the dry fly when appropriate, but as Pritt correctly pointed out, it can be an unrewarding pastime on rivers where trout for a large part of the season do not freely rise. From the authors' experience, casting a dry fly over water with no rising fish is rather pointless, and one can have much better sport by adopting the North Country Fishing Style.

North Country fly patterns

'North Country patterns' is a general term given to a group of flies that have a very soft and mobile hackle. The body of the fly is often simply made of one or two layers of coloured thread or dubbing. North Country wet flies are often very sparsely dressed, with as little as one or two turns of soft game or poultry hackle. They tend to have a slim body of silk and fur, extending to a position no further along the shank than opposite the barb of the hook.

The salient feature of the North County patterns is their versatility in being able to represent various life-cycle development stages of insects, including nymphs, still born duns, adult duns and spinners. Whether the patterns are fished on, in, or just below the surface, the dressings appear to be suggestive of various forms of fly life.

Before 1800 many fly patterns incorporated a winged dressing, however, after this date hackled flies began to appear in lists of flies. It is commonly believed that the hackled fly derived from the palmer flies (Lawrie, 1969; Fogg, 1988). Palmered dressings are thought to represent various caterpillars, illustrations of which appear in the earliest angling literature. After the palmers came the 'half-palmered' hackle flies in which the hackle is only wound part way down the body. Half-palmered flies were commonly used on Devon and Derbyshire rivers and became known as 'bumbles' or dressed 'buzz'. The traditional North Country hackled patterns appear to be a logical development of the half-palmered fly, the final transition being the substitution of hen, game or soft bird feathers for the traditional cock hackle.

W. H. Lawrie suggested in tying a North Country pattern the fly-dresser should practice artistic restraint in the application of any material as seems reasonably possible. The North Country patterns seldom incorporate a tail or wings as these elements add nothing to the effectiveness of a spate river fly. As H. C. Cutcliffe noted in his book, *Trout Fishing on Rapid Streams*, the current manipulates a winged fly and makes the fly move unrealistically and also without stability. The soft mobile hackle was specifically chosen to represent both the wings and the legs of an insect and to provide maximum mobility, which becomes reduced as soon as wings are added to a fly.

Several well known soft-hackled wet fly North Country patterns are named conveniently and simply by referring to the colour of its body and the name of the bird which provided the hackle feather. These patterns included the Green Woodcock, Orange Partridge, Red Grouse, and Snipe and Purple. It is noteable that some of the North Country patterns are referred to as 'Bloas', for example the Waterhen Bloa or Poult Bloa. The word Bloa is a description of the hackle feather's inky-grey or slate-blue colour. Bloa patterns, therefore, possess a dull blue-grey hackle, often found on the wing of a coot, waterhen or starling. Other famous Bloa patterns included Dark Bloa, Starling Bloa and Yellow Legged Bloa.

Many of these North Country patterns originate from Yorkshire and Derbyshire, however, other soft-hackled patterns have origins in Lancashire, the Lake District, the North East, Scotland and North Wales. These flies were frequently referred to in the angling press as 'North Country' patterns after 1886 when T. E. Pritt's *Yorkshire Trout Flies* was re-published as *North Country Flies*. It should be noted that the North Country fly patterns appear to have little in common with the Scottish 'spider' patterns and indeed they represent a quite separate line of development. Several lists of North Country fly patterns for use on the River Wharfe have been made dating back to the late 1700s; some of these are listed after the bibliographical references in this book. Perhaps the best known lists are those of Sylvester Lister or Pritt. Sylvester Lister's list was later copied by Edmonds and Lee (1916). In 1873 Sylvester Lister was a founder member of what is now called the Appletreewick, Barden and Burnsall Angling Club; he is buried at Bolton Abbey.

Three of the most successful flies for use on the River Wharfe are included on Sylvester Lister's list; these are the Partridge and Orange, Snipe and Purple, and Waterhen Bloa. They are usually dressed on hook sizes 14 and 16. The Partridge and Orange is sometimes tied on a larger size 12 hook.

Choosing which flies to use

William Brumfitt, the famous Otley fly-fisherman had a large collection of flies and he recorded their peculiarities and the times of the year when they should be used. However, when talking to a representative from the *Fishing Gazette* during the late 1800s, he said, 'Yet that is not always reliable, for I have often found that March flies will kill in April and May, and even up to June and so on. The best guide is for a fisherman to go to the river and see what flies are on, and then act accordingly. At one time I used to go down to the river and watch the flies carefully, and then tie a few on the river bank. But I have found that did not pay, as the time spent tying flies ought to have been given to fishing.'

The size and colour of the fly is therefore an important factor. The secret is 'knowing' what the natural fly is on the water and choosing the fly that most closely resembles that fly in colour and size, an observation also noted by Sylvester Lister. For example, in selecting some wet fly patterns, one of the easiest choices is the Partridge and Yellow in a 14 or 16 when a medium olive or olive upright hatch is on. A Partridge and Orange may be used when the dominant insect might be one of the larger *Ephemeropteran* such as the blue winged olive. A Partridge and Green may be used when the dominant trout food might be the darker caddis or *Baetis*. A black and white soft-hackled pattern in size 20 is a good choice when you are fishing during a hatch of tiny midges, possibly during the evening.

Some anglers contend that the Partridge and Orange is taken for an adult stonefly or the aquatic nymph of this species. Other fisherman said this is a general pattern used to represent nymphs of a range of up-wing species. Others assert that the orange body is used to imitate a developing midge pupa. Another famous North Country pattern is the Waterhen Bloa; anglers purport that its colour, size and behaviour in flowing water suggest a member of the olive family either struggling to hatch or possibly drowning in the process of hatching. The straggly body and soft pliable hackle of the Waterhen Bloa is designed specifically to quiver and flutter in the current. The Waterhen Bloa still catches fish when not a single member of the olive family is present on the Wharfe. A number of angling authorities have asserted that the Snipe and Purple is a dressing to represent the nymph or adult iron blue dun. However, it should be noted that the iron blue dun seldom hatches to any extent on the River Wharfe today. Despite this the Snipe and Purple continues to catch fish wherever it is used on the Wharfe.

It is also important to note that throughout a particular hatch of flies it is sometimes worth ringing the changes as sometimes the fish will go off the winged flies entirely and become selective to the emergers and floating nymphs. For example, during a hatch of olive duns it may be worth fishing a *Baetis* nymph deep an hour before the hatch starts when the nymphs are beginning to move and the trout are just picking up on them; then switch to the emerger or floating nymph as the hatch builds up. A dry fly can then be used late in the emergence when there are no more nymphs left and the trout are picking out the last of the duns. At the end of the hatch it may be worth using a dry spent-wing or spinner pattern on those sporadic, late risers that are taking crippled duns in the backwaters or eddies. It is therefore important that the fly fisherman remains observant throughout the day and changes his/ her fly to 'match the hatch' and imitate the creatures on which the trout and grayling are feeding on.

As Pat O'Reilly (2003) aptly wrote, 'Matching the hatch by using an artificial fly sufficiently similar to the creatures on which the trout are feeding can greatly increase your chances of success. That is not to suggest it is every day on every river and lake that the trout feed in a selective way; sometimes all that the fish are looking for is food, and then just about any fly fished in a realistic way will do the job. But when trout are being selective they may lock on to one particular type of insect – perhaps even to just one stage in the life-cycle of that insect – and then Lady Luck smiles upon the angler who uses the right fly, fishes it in the right place and makes it behave like the natural insect.'

Reading the river

Before describing the methods of fishing North Country patterns, it is important to note that when wet fly-fishing it is necessary for the angler to read the river intelligently. For example, when fishing a river in spring it is worth remembering Pritt's advice, 'Cast your flies as much as possible to the side of the river towards which the wind blows; the natural insects are blown thither and the trout are there.' In spring when trout are in poor condition and recovering from the winter and spawning, they tend to prefer areas of the river where there are pools, or a gentle flow of 2-3 feet deep water, and where the bank is close by. This location is enhanced further with the presence of overhanging trees which provide shade and a supply of terrestrial insects and other fauna for the trout.

On gaining their strength and as the temperature of the water increases during the season, the trout can then negotiate the stronger currents and oxygenated waters in search of food. During the summer, trout can be found feeding in the shallow water and adjacent to strong currents, fast pools and eddies. Towards the end of the season, the trout begin to search the areas near to the inlets of spawning becks. Fishing lore says trout 'know' that winter is coming and things will be getting very tough soon, so they stock up, putting on fat. What happens in the months before the season begins may well control the behaviour of the trout, their condition, and favoured lies. These factors are inter-related and to a large extent controlled by the weather.

During the early season it should be remembered that, 'it's never much good on the Wharfe in an upstream wind' (notes by T. E. Pritt (1887), Magee (1994)). It is true that a cold easterly wind, particularly during low level water early in the season, does not provide good conditions for fly-fishing. However, according to T. E. Pritt's observations, during the summer months an upstream wind may be beneficial for fishing, as it tends to 'keep the feed on, and as long as there is food upon the water, trout are on the look-out for it'.

During April, easterly winds combined with clear low water make fishing conditions extremely difficult. When wading in clear water, trout are easily spooked. T. E. Pritt noted during April 1887, 'The river is so woefully bright and clear under the combined effects of the east wind and steely atmosphere, with the usual accompaniment of a cloudless sky, that only a few of the most accomplished hands can hope to get more than half-a-dozen trout as a result of a hard day's work under such conditions' (Magee, 1994).

Dick Routledge a fly-fisher of the River Eden said 'fish the froth', an old tip for rough streams that can be recommended: 'Where there is a deep hole with shelter and some froth there will usually be a good trout.' Trout sometimes lie under accumulations of froth as flies often get trapped within the froth (notes from T. E. Pritt (1884), Magee (1994)).

General North Country Style fishing methods

William Brumfitt recognised the importance of presentation and the way the fly is fished to achieve success: 'I am fishing with the same flies on the Wharfe now to those I fished with 60 years ago, and I always will. Much depends on the way the flies are used.'

The fly-fisher should start fishing the head of the riffle, only wading on the shallow side if necessary and fishing the deeper or holding water on the other side. The best kind of riffle for this kind of fishing will be quite streamy or open with medium speed across the breadth of the river.

The line, leader, and fly should come downstream as one, to give an even, natural look to the fly. Cast across and slightly down stream, and let the line and leader move downstream at the speed of the current. Try to cast a loose line, not a tight one. In some areas it may be possible to follow the line down with the rod tip held high. This helps to set the hook when the fish takes the fly, although in most cases the trout hook themselves in this style of fishing. Sometimes the rod may be held higher to prevent drag where the speed of flow decreases across the river. Do not jerk the line, thinking this will make the flies more appealing. The distance of the drift should not be too long, about 30 degrees. The best takes are in the upper part of the drift where the fish sees the whole side of the fly.

Move down the riffle a step or two at a time, cast again, and repeat the process for the length of the riffle. As you move down the riffle, follow the line with the rod tip held high to keep line-drag to a minimum and to be able to react quickly to a take or rise to the fly. Vary the casting distance if you need it and fish the swim thoroughly. Also keep an eye out for fish close to the path you're taking downstream. Often, you will find more speed between you and the fly, creating a belly in the line, which causes the line and fly to drag across the current in a very unnatural manner. The drag can be eliminated by mending the line (i.e. rolling the line over as you would jump a rope).

When using a soft-hackled fly it should be noted that the fly adjusts itself to the action of the water. The leaders and lines used, therefore, must be as fine as possible to allow the fly to naturally adjust to the current. In order to present the fly slowly to the fish, it is important that the angler controls the speed of the fly by the cast and the subsequent mending of the line by the raised manipulation of the rod and line to prevent drag effects on the fly.

Downstream wet fly-fishing

One traditional method of North Country style fly-fishing is to cast the flies across and downstream at an angle of 45 degrees to the bank. This technique is known as 'downstream' wet fly-fishing. The rod is held high and the line and cast allowed to move downstream with minimal drag in a slight arc towards the near bank. A fish taking the fly may be observed by a straightening of the line, or may be felt as a distinct tug on the line. When the line has completed its arc downstream the flies begin to rise in the water; this often induces the fish to take.

The leaders used for downstream wet fly-fishing are generally about 9ft long, with relatively light tippets so that the leader is limp enough for a good drift, but still strong enough to play a decent-size trout with some authority. Some fly-fishermen are not convinced that trout actually see a heavier leader and become spooked. Some believe they either don't see the leader at all, or that they see it clearly, but don't care about it one way or another. What they 'do' care about is how natural the drift of the fly is. Your trout fly should be helplessly bobbing along on every crease and ripple of the water because that's what the real insects around it are doing and fish pay close attention to these things.

On completing the cast and fishing the flies as described the angler should then move a couple of steps downstream repeating the process, thereby, covering and 'searching' for fish throughout the run.

A certain amount of skill is required to control the flies as they traverse the stream or river. It is important to guide the flies and the point of the rod must be moved across the stream in advance of them. This technique is called 'leading the flies' and results in the cast being fished more slowly across the current and the flies will travel both across and downstream at the same time. A cast across the current and the rod being held at 45 degrees to the bank without movement of the rod to 'lead the flies' will result in the flies moving across the current with increasing pace and drag on the leader and flies. This will result in the unnatural presentation of the flies and possibly disturb fish present in the run. Once the wet fly fisherman has gained confidence in this technique, they can give the fish a little more line which will reduce drag further, however, this will make it more difficult to detect bites. This can be done by keeping the rod held high and allowing some slack line between the rod tip and stream.

Upstream and across stream fishing

Another wet fly technique is known as 'upstream and across' stream fishing. Edmonds and Lee (1916) described this method as follows: 'The angler faces the bank towards which he proposes fishing, casts across and slightly upstream, then allows the flies to be carried without drag till they reach a point a few yards below where they alighted upon the water. Wading downstream a yard or more, he repeats the cast, until the whole stream has been worked in this manner.'

This technique allows the flies to drift several metres below the angler's position with minimal drag on the flies. This method also allows the flies to be seen by a fish in advance of the line. A team of three flies may be fished at various depths thereby maximising the chances of selecting the correct depth and pattern of fly which the fish are taking.

In order to avoid drag, which will cause the flies to skate unnaturally across the river, the line can be cast with a snakey line by flicking the rod quickly downstream and upstream at the end of the cast, or a line with an upstream bow in it by making a sharp flick of the rod tip in an upstream direction when the cast is completed. To ensure that the flies float down the river at a natural pace, the angler should mend the line by drawing out extra line from the reel and pay it out as required. As soon as a downstream bow becomes visible, the line should be mended by a little roll of the rod in an upstream direction so that the bow is transferred to an upstream position.

When the line has completed its downstream drift, the flies can then be allowed to swing across the current, the rod tip guiding them; the flies will subsequently rise in the water. This action can be deadly as the flies suggest the movement of an ascending nymph and trout often take the fly as it rises through the water. It is therefore important to fish out each cast very carefully as trout may take flies towards the end of the drift.

If no fish takes, the line should be retrieved gently until it is safe to re-cast without disturbing the surface and possibly scaring the fish. The line can be mended easily using a long soft-action rod and a supple floating line. A soft-action rod will cast with a wide loop which is essential when avoiding tangles with a three-fly cast and will also allow the angler to roll cast when there are high river banks or trees and bushes behind.

There has been some debate on when to use the downstream method or upstream and across method. Arthur Ransome (1980) said that downstream fishing should be used when the river is high and fast-flowing. Edmonds and Lee (1916) suggested that the downstream method should be 'confined to strong and full waters, to waters tinged with colour, to cold spring days before and after the hatch, to evening fishing in such places as have the river flowing towards the sunset, and, lastly, to occasions when a heavy downstream wind or the nature of the country leaves the angler no choice.'

T. E. Pritt (1886) said that: 'Everything depends upon the size of the river, the condition of the water, and the nature of the bait. To fish upstream is an unnecessary labour in a discoloured water and to fish downstream in a clear water is to court both disappointment and ridicule; for, in the latter case, except in a turbulent eddy or broken rapid, the angler will be perfectly visible to every fish for many a good yard below him.'

The fly should be fished downstream when fish lie in the cushion of slack water which forms upstream of a restriction such as a large boulder, bridge pier, or at the head of a weed bed. Fish at such locations are difficult to reach with an upstream cast because of the risk of snagging the flies or lining the fish. When fish are present in wide streamy shallows a downstream approach should be taken. A downstream cast with plenty of slack line being paid off the reel should be used to enable the fly to drift freely down to the fish in a natural manner. This method means that the trout, fly, line and angler lie in a straight line and the fish will only see the fly drifting down to it as any natural insect floating just beneath the surface film. Fish tend to take the fly confidently when fished in this manner. J.W. Hills (author of *A History of Fly-Fishing for Trout*) recognised that this method was effective when fish are difficult to catch on low water: 'Good fishermen, on the shyest of waters, fish downstream and kill fish.'

However, some anglers have been critical about the downstream method. For example, W. C. Stewart (1857) argued that an angler will be seen when fishing downstream since the trout generally faces upstream. He also said that the fly may be pulled more easily from the trout's mouth when it is lying in a downstream position. Fly-fisherman using the downstream method have often said that, when fishing the upstream method, more skill is required in controlling the flies, and in discerning the take. A constant mending of the line is also necessary in order to keep in touch with the flies. In fast water it is necessary to retrieve the line very quickly with the free hand whilst keeping the rod high.

When fishing the upstream method it is easier to use frequent short casts, keeping the rod high and looking for the slightest indication of a taking trout. Most of the North Country patterns are light in construction and when fished upstream tend to be close to the surface. In this position the fish considers the fly to resemble either an ascending mature nymph or a drowned adult fly. In some cases it may be useful to degrease the leader so that the line is beneath the surface and less likely to scare the fish. Upstream wet fly-fishing usually involves wading; when wading enter the water gently and move slowly so not to disturb fish close by.

It is best to cast upstream first before casting upstream and across as this is likely to disturb more fish. The greatest problem of fishing directly upstream is that it is easy to 'line' fish by casting over them. A short upstream cast should therefore be used first of all and the area near to you should be 'searched' first of all. A short cast using a long rod will enable the flies to be controlled easily as they drift back towards you. As the flies drift back towards you, a progressive raising of the rod will keep the angler in touch with the flies and will ensure a natural drift. It is important to be disciplined and use short casts (i.e. 1½ times the rod length) and not be tempted to use a longer cast and line fish in the process. In using a short cast it is easier to see a taking fish. Using a short cast together with a longer rod held high will also allow most of the line to be kept off the water and the angler can easily control the flies. The use of light fly lines is also beneficial for upstream wet fly fishing.

Having searched the water thoroughly directly upstream, the angler can then cast upstream and across gradually extending the upstream cast until the whole width of the stream has been explored. It is important to mend the line as soon as a bow develops in the line when casting upstream and across. It is important that the drift of the flies remains as natural as possible. One way an experienced fly-caster can use is to cast the line with an upstream bow in it while the flies land downstream of the bow. The line must be continuously mended to prolong the free drift of the flies. A longer rod held high is again useful to make upstream and downstream mends to the line with minimal effort. Wet fly-fishing upstream therefore demands hard work and concentration in order to control the way the flies are fished. The upstream method also allows the top dropper fly to be fished as a 'bob fly' so that it can skip along the surface like a natural insect. The palmered North Country patterns are a perfect fly to fish in this manner. Fish can be taken very close to the angler and therefore the flies should be fished as close as possible before recasting.

It is necessary to be constantly on the move and to wade upstream and across the stream in order to search every possible lie, including little runs, eddies, channels and slack water behind boulders. Searching the water in this way is the obvious approach when there are no fish rising and is the classic North Country method. The river should be fished systematically, crossing and re-crossing, each time a few metres higher up, until the whole length of water has been covered. The upstream method requires patience and stealth, moving gently and quietly so not to disturb fish close by.

Grayling fishing on the River Wharfe

The River Wharfe could be considered more of a trout river than the Ure or the Nidd, but it does have good stocks of grayling in places, particularly from Ilkley downstream, and in decreasing numbers upstream of Ilkley. The grayling in the upper River Wharfe have declined over the last 20 years. The area around Burnsall once had very large stocks, but, although they are still present, they are not there in the same numbers.

The Burnsall section from Barden Bridge through to the stepping stones at Bolton Abbey holds good trout and grayling and is a lovely mix of water with some great tail pools for the dry fly. The water upstream of Appletreewick, where the little peat-stained River Dibb runs in, holds some good fish; as does the stretch above Loup Scar and the water above the Hebden Suspension Bridge. Fly-fishers wanting to fish for grayling should try the stretch of river at Bolton Abbey below the A59 bridge starting at the Lob Pool and fish upstream to Ferry House Reach. Also the water around the Cavendish Pavilion and then up into the Strid can produce good sport. However, casting through Strid Wood requires care. Further downstream in Mid Wharfedale, the section of the Wharfe upstream of the Pool-in-Wharfedale road bridge provides some excellent grayling fishing.

The grayling fly-fishing extends the fly-fisher's year on the River Wharfe right through autumn and winter. In effect this gives the fly-fisherman only 10 days, from 15 March to 24 March (North Yorkshire Close) when anglers are unable to fish the rivers for brown trout or grayling. However, the best time of the year for grayling fly-fishing is from September to December when they are at their most active and feeding hard throughout the day. The dry fly-fishing during early autumn when grayling are rising to the Autumn Dun and Pale Wateries can be very good. However, the speed of the grayling rise can often lead to frustration. It is well worth prospecting some tails and riffles with a dry/nymph combination. This method has been used for over a hundred years on the Wharfe. On the end of a 9ft tapered cast, tie on one of Jim Wynn's bushy dry flies (or a Klinkhammer) recommended for grayling. Then tie a short 18 inch piece of tippet (6X is fine) to the bend of the dry fly and tie on a small bead headed nymph. For example a Pheasant Tail with a tiny tungsten bead on a size 16 or 18 hook. This klink and dunk method can be lethal when fished with a relatively short line and working upstream, fan-casting as you go. The short line allows you to counteract the current and ensures that the flies fish dead drift; even a touch of drag will render the method ineffective. For such tactics lightweight rods and lines pay dividends. The grayling in particular will usually respond to these subtle tactics and a softer approach than those used for the brown trout.

The dry fly-fishing begins to decline in December and the fly-fisher needs to employ different methods to catch grayling on the bottom of the river. With the onset of the colder winter weather the fly-fisher can use the Czech nymphing or bugging technique or possibly the 'duo' or 'trio' methods to get the flies down to the zone where the grayling lie. In such conditions it is important to search every pool thoroughly to find the winter grayling, using river craft and experience to determine where they will be lying. Grayling are an ideal quarry for the inexperienced fly-fisher as they are more tolerant of an angler's presence than the brown trout; in broken water they can be caught very near to the angler. Unlike the brown trout they will not bolt for cover at the first sight of an angler, but generally move away slowly whilst continuing to feed.

Please note that barbless hooks should be used on the days ticket waters of the River Wharfe. A word of caution apart from flattening the barbs: grayling in particular can take small size fly patterns well back, so forceps are also handy to extract flies from their tiny mouths.

3 Some notable fly-fishermen of the River Wharfe

Apart from the known authors of fishing books written between 1750 and 1850 there are few records made by fly-fishermen who fished the River Wharfe during this period. This is unfortunate because the North Country patterns do owe their development to generations of forgotten anglers who lived and fished in Wharfedale. John Waller Hills (1921) said that every angler who had fished for a generation or longer should write down their recollections of their fishing exploits. This will leave a record of the state of things for following angling generations to cogitate over. North and West Yorkshire has had a long and fine tradition of fly-fishing; here is a brief review of some of the more notable fly-fishers that fished the River Wharfe.

William Pilling (1733-1807) who was the corn-miller at Pool-in-Wharfedale must have been an accomplished fly-fisher of the River Wharfe. He produced one of the earliest known historical lists of flies for use on the River Wharfe. John Swarbrick also must have been an observant and knowledgeable fly-fisher of the River Wharfe and produced *Swarbrick's List of Flies for the River Wharfe* in 1807. J. W. Sagar of Ilkley was a well known Wharfedale angler whose dressing, Sagar's Fancy, still appears in lists of North Country river flies. J. W. Sagar's fly dressings appeared with John Swarbrick's list of dressings published by E. Beanlands in 1907. John Swarbrick was a farmer and farmed land near High and Low Austby. He fished the River Wharfe at Middleton, Ilkley, Ben Rhydding and Denton. Jerome Emmott was noted to be a well known fly-tyer and fly-fisherman of Kilnsey and was a contemporary of Swarbrick and Sagar. William Pickard was also a farmer at High Austby and knew Swarbrick. His son John Pickard produced another list of flies for the River Wharfe in 1820. He also fished the same stretches of the River Wharfe as Swarbrick.

T. C. Hofland, author of *The British Angler's Manual* (1839), often fished the River Wharfe and stayed at the shooting lodge at Bolton Priory as a guest of the Duke of Devonshire. He travelled all over England as a landscape painter but also spent a considerable time fishing for trout on the Wharfe. Hofland included in his list of 46 flies, several hackle fly dressings which were typical of the hackle flies preferred in the North of England. Hofland was one of the first writers to describe how a hackle fly should be dressed. There are accounts of Hofland catching a trout of 4lb (caught on minnow not fly) at Harewood Bridge on the River Wharfe.

T. H. Barker of Hoveringham in North Yorkshire was noted to be a competent fly-fisher and fished the Wharfe. Barker was responsible for editing and publishing John Jackson's manuscript, *The Practical Fly-Fisher, More Particularly for Grayling or Umber* (1853) after Jackson's death in 1853. The dressings of Jackson along with Theakston have long been regarded as standard fly patterns for the River Wharfe and River Ure where they lived. Michael Theakston, author of *A List of Natural Flies* (1853), lived by the River Skell in Ripon. His fly dressings were widely used on both the River Wharfe and River Ure.

Henry Cadman, author of *Harry Druidale, Fisherman from Manxland to England*, (1897) wrote about fishing on the higher Kilnsey reaches of the Wharfe during the 1880s. Contemporary with him, and frequenting the much longer stretches downstream of Kilnsey through Grassington, Burnsall, Barden, Ilkley and Otley, were some of Yorkshire's most polished exponents of wet fly-fishing.

Joshua Hart (1841-1909), who was born in Otley and who was a successful Bradford businessman, was one of very few North Country fishermen that kept a diary. He not only fished the Otley and Ilkley reaches in his younger days, but was a member of the Appletreewick, Barden and Burnsall Angling Club from 1878 until his death in 1909. In 1891 Joshua Hart on a fishing holiday to the River Skirfare filled his basket every day on Gold-ribbed Poult and Green, Dark Needle and Orange and Partridge. On another visit to the Skirfare his companion caught many trout on the Brazzle (starling quill wing, purple silk body, hackle of blood-red on black). In a notebook he jotted down his reminiscences, experiences and some pertinent observations of the fly-fishing skill of those who were his contemporaries. Joshua Hart wrote about a fly-fisherman called Willie Binns. Binns frequented the Burnsall stretches of the River Wharfe and often took 50 fish on many trips. On a day on the Kilnsey Club's waters, his avowed intention was to creel 100 trout; he just managed to top the 90 mark.

Joshua Hart also wrote about a fly-fisherman called John Willie, who had fished the River Wharfe from being a lad. John Willie was a keen observer of nature, and knew what species of aquatic fly life to expect with the changes in atmospheric conditions. 'When fish were to be got on the fly, he could get them, and he got them at times when no one else could.' He often fished the Smoke Fly (grouse poult hackle and peacock herl body). Joshua Hart records that 'John Willie worked wonders with the Smoke Fly when the river was low. His Poult Bloa, Light Watchet, Light Needle and Light Ant, killed him a lot of fish on summer evenings, when he regularly took from 15 to 25. He had good sight and was a first class night fisher. He was right in any water, generally fished up, and could use his flies as he liked.'

Another fly fisherman that thought highly of the Smoke Fly and the Needle patterns was Sylvester Lister of Barden Tower. Joshua Hart ranked Lister as a first-rate fly-fisherman and a keen observer of aquatic flies and the haunts of trout. Although some would say he dressed a clumsy fly, they still deceived the trout. Sylvester Lister (1821-1900) lived at Barden Tower near Bolton Abbey for sixty years. He combined his farming with river keeping for the Bolton Abbey Estate. According to Francis Walbran, who knew him well, Lister was regarded as the 'father' of the Wharfedale fly-fishers. He was a founder member of the Appletreewick, Barden and Burnsall Angling Club in 1873, which still controls much of the Wharfe for several miles upstream of Barden.

Lister believed in having the right fly, and was very exact when selecting the size and colour of dressings for certain conditions. Lister invariably caught well with his Light Needle (inside starling, orange silk and mauve head). Sylvester Lister used to say, 'When swallows come, look out for the Olive Bloa, Dark Watchet, Orange Partridge, Light Needle, Little Black and Moor Game. When you notice the wagtails, it is time to use the Stone Midge'. Lister was contemptuous of the well to do anglers who came to the Wharfe with three or four flies on their cast saying, 'They are too lazy to find out what the fish and the birds are doing, if they watched the water and the seasons they would catch more fish with one fly than they ever do now with four.'

During his fishing career he kept the exact details of his regular dressings undisclosed, but towards the end he was persuaded by several of his close friends to write down his list of traditional patterns for the Wharfe. He produced a list of dressings *List of artificial flies used by Silvester Lister Snr, Barden Tower, nr Bolton Abbey* (1898). One or two other copies were made from the original by Sylvester's son, and the patterns were considered to be so deadly that the recipients were sworn to secrecy. Sylvester Lister's list of flies is in fact largely derived from John Swarbrick's *List of Flies for the River Wharfe* (1807); several dressings bear the same list number as Swarbrick's. It should also be noted that Edmonds and Lee, in their book *Brook and River Trouting* (1916), included most of Lister's dressings without any acknowledgment to Lister or Swarbrick.

Lister's friend, Park Inman, was very successful in using the Stone Midge dressing, which he fished singly on sunny afternoons. Willie Birch was another who killed many trout on the Stone Midge; he also took many a basket on the Knotted Midge pattern.

George Deamine once took 38 trout from the River Skirfare at Hawkswick on a fly without moving his stance. He always used a Partridge and Crimson on his cast early in the season. When the trout were difficult he always tried them with a grass-green bodied Partridge.

Tommy Thompson was another expert fly-fisher, who always used an Orange Partridge when the dark needle was out in large numbers, and whose favourite for summer-night fly-fishing was a Sea Swallow or a very light Poult with peacock herl body.

George Hoyle, another successful fly-fisher who fished the Wharfe regularly liked a Poult and Pea Green for night fishing, a Poult and Orange or Blue Snipe for Whitsuntide, a Fieldfare Rump, with ostrich herl head and body, for the back-end, and a Fieldfare with lead-coloured body ribbed with cowslip silk for the opening days.

It is interesting to note that in Joshua Hart's notebook he made the following entry: 'We are now in 1906, and we hear much of the old hands and what they did, but where there were five on the water there are a hundred today. On the Burnsall length in 1905 a thousand rods were out.' It would appear that in Joshua Hart's day, fly hatches were a good deal more prolific on the Wharfe, but the artificials he mentions will still hold their own when the naturals, in the likeness of which they are fashioned, are showing.

Francis Darwin of Creskeld Hall, Arthington, who owned the local fishing rights on the River Wharfe, writing *circa* 1860 said that: 'Twenty years ago there lived at Arthington, Christopher Spence, a dealer in pots and an extremely excellent fly-fisherman, throwing a fly with great skill. The River Wharfe was full of fish, a few salmon and barbell but plenty of others. We speared the barbell as we did salmon … Smelt used to be netted in Otley, placed on a sheet before the White Horse and sold by the gallon measure.'

Old Bradley of Otley was a well known fly-tyer and fly-fisherman in Otley during the mid 1800s. At this time the River Wharfe at Otley attracted many famous anglers including Sir Humphry Davy, the great scientist and much travelled fly-fisher, and William Turner, the famous landscape painter, during his annual stay at Farnley Hall near Otley.

William Brumfitt (1846-1926) was the senior member of the Otley School of fly-fishers and had a huge influence on T. E. Pritt when he moved to

Yorkshire. William Brumfitt was the grandson of Timothy Thackeray, one of the most noted of Wharfedale fishermen. His uncle was Ned Thackeray also a well known fisherman of the River Wharfe. These two men must have had a strong influence on William Brumfitt from an early age. William Brumfitt was the mentor of T. E. Pritt and tied most of the flies for the engravings in Pritt's *Yorkshire Trout Flies.*

Brumfitt was an exceptional fly-fisherman who caught thousands of trout on a single fished fly, the hooks all whipped to horsehair. His record for one season was 2,000 trout; this is approximately 11 fish a day for a typical trout season from April to September. It is documented that he never fished with a rod or a fly that was not of his own making. Brumfitt would walk from Otley to Ilkley to fish the River Wharfe at Ilkley as a young man, as there was no railway at that time. Brumfitt was a close friend and fishing companion of W. Carter Platts and also counted amongst his friends the following notable Wharfe anglers: William Kendall, William Hawksworth, Joseph Moon, William Critchley, S. Kendall and 'Owd Delves.' Brumfitt was a notable professional fly-tyer and never departed from the North Country patterns; however, he was also convinced that presentation was the major part of fly-fishing skill.

William Brumfitt was also fond of shooting, however, he had no delusions as to which was the better sport. 'Fishing,' he used to say, 'brings everyone to one level. I don't care how wealthy a man is, an angler has no better chance than any other. Now in shooting birds, the game – the pheasants, the partridge or whatever they might be – are driven towards the guns and all you have to do is shoot. But with fishing it is different, no matter how wealthy a man is he cannot drive the fish to the bait; he can't make them bite if they don't want to do so. If they did a poor man would get no fishing.'

W. Carter Platts (1858-1944) was one of the best known writers about angling in Yorkshire, (*Modern Trout Fishing,* 1938). He filled hundreds of columns in the *Yorkshire Post* and its weekly edition for many years, contributed extensively to the sporting press, wrote half a dozen books about angling which may be favourably compared to modern works and became a novelist. He lived in Kettlewell in 1902 and fished the River Wharfe at this time. He fished with C. J. Cutcliffe Hyne, who also lived in Kettlewell. He moved to Skipton in 1916 and lived there until he died in 1944. Carter Platts knew and fished with Alfred Holden Illingworth of Otley (1869-1935). Illingworth was a textile worker who became a tackle dealer, and he regularly fly-fished the River Wharfe; however, he was better known as the inventor of the Illingworth Reel patented in 1905 and a pioneer of the fixed spool reel. Jim Bazeley, a schoolmaster from Leeds, was a well known fly-fisherman who fished the Wharfe with Carter Platts at the turn of the 19th Century. Illingworth, Bazeley, and Carter Platts often tried out Illingworth's reels on the Wharfe at Otley for trout. Carter Platts was also a close fly-fishing companion of William Brumfitt. Carter Platts' work *Grayling Fishing* (1939), is one of the most readable books on the subject.

Richard M. Pratt (1827-1917) had a chemist shop in Otley. He was a close friend of Walbran and Brumfitt and became a notable fly-fisher. He became the secretary of Otley Angling Club in 1873. Pratt was best known for being the first individual to rear trout in Yorkshire. Pratt became interested in Frank Buckland's experiments in fish culture in the 1860s and began rearing trout by stripping spawning fish taken in local tributaries. He was so successful that he made a small hatchery in outhouses behind his shop and was soon turning large numbers of fingerlings into the Wharfe. Within 3 to 4 years the Otley length was reputed to be second only to Driffield for the number and size of brown trout in its preserves and the club became very exclusive. Within a few years, trout hatcheries and hatching boxes were installed on most North

County rivers and ova, fry and young trout were introduced to the river.

Thomas Evan Pritt (1848-1895) achieved his place in the annals of fly-fishing literature through his two best known books, *The Book of the Grayling* and *North-Country Flies*. *The Book of the Grayling* for its sincerity and its enthusiasm and *North-Country Flies* because it described the type of fly in use at that time on the rivers and streams of northern England, and included hand coloured plates of each of the flies. Pritt made no claim for originality in the actual dressings of the 62 flies in his book, indeed he went to great lengths to acknowledge the

Thomas Evan Pritt (1848-1895)

generous help given by his many angling friends. The flies in the book were tied by two professional fly-tyers, William Brumfitt of Otley and Jerome Emmott of Kilnsey. T. E. Pritt died at the age of 47 from influenza.

T. E. Pritt's recommended casts were as follows:

1. *March to the end of April* Tail fly Broughton's Point, first dropper Waterhen Bloa, second dropper Woodcock, third dropper Dark Snipe.

2. *Middle of April to end of June* Tail fly March Brown, first dropper Snipe Bloa, second dropper Iron Blue Dun, third dropper Orange Partridge.

3. *Middle or end of June onwards* Tail fly, Brown Owl, first dropper Poult Bloa, second dropper Knotted Midge, third dropper Yellow May Dun.

Pritt also suggested that in September the first cast may be used, varying it if occasion arises with either Dark Needle, Fog Black or Brown Owl.

Francis 'Max' Walbran (1852-1909) was born in Ripon. He moved to Leeds where he was a chemist's manager. He lived at Ivy Cottage in Pool-in-Wharfedale from 1883 to his death. He began to write articles for the *Fishing Gazette* from the time it was founded in 1876 when he was only 24 years old and continued to write until his death in 1909. He was a notable grayling angler and published the book *Grayling and How to Catch Them*, (1895).

He regularly fished the River Ure and formed the Tanfield Angling Club in 1887. He was also closely associated with R. M. Pratt and T. E. Pritt, and they all belonged to the Appletreewick, Barden and Burnsall Angling Club. Walbran set up a fishing tackle shop in Leeds at 19 Station Street. He continued to be a fishing tackle dealer until his death. During the 10 years in Pool he corresponded with many famous anglers. Among them were R. B. Marston, editor of the *Fishing Gazette*, W. Senior ('Red Spinner') of the *Field*, F. M. Halford of dry fly fame, C. H. Cook ('John Bickerdyke'), Francis Francis, Marriott, Sherringham and other stalwarts of the game

Frances Walbran (1852-1909)

fishing world of his day. Walbran was also adept at upstream worming on the River Wharfe near Pool. Besides Walbran's prolific contributions to angling journals and newspapers he republished Theakston's *A List of Natural Flies* (1853) under the title of *The British Angler* (1889) with some additional chapters. In Yorkshire he is perhaps best known for popularising the Red Tag, which was shown to him by a Worcestershire angler who was visiting the River Ure in 1878. Max Walbran was drowned on 15 February 1909 at the age of 57 whilst grayling fishing at West Tanfield on the Ure, in a rapidly rising river. He was buried in West Tanfield churchyard.

F. M. Walbran's favourite patterns were as follows: Waterhen Bloa, Dark Snipe and Purple, Snipe Bloa, Partridge and Orange, Bracken Clock (summer), and Stone Midge (summer). He also recommended the following flies: Spanish Needle (summer and autumn); Winter Brown (spring and autumn); Dark Snipe and Orange (spring and autumn); Blue Partridge (April and May); Fog Black (summer and autumn); Grey Midge (summer); Apple-green Dun (autumn); August Dun (late summer).

Tom Chippendale was born in Otley and was believed to be a descendant of Thomas Chippendale the famous cabinet maker also of Otley. He became an expert fly-fisher on the Wharfe at Otley and also tied flies professionally. His flies were renowned for the resilience of the horse hair to which they were whipped. Brumfitt passed on to Chippendale his cherished pattern book, probably in the early 1900s. To this book, Chippendale added a list of 'Otley Standard Flies' and a number of dry flies, mostly from the Halford series. In his regular angling reports which continued in the local press until around 1940 he usually recommended a few 'killing' patterns of wet flies for the current conditions but never once mentioned the dry fly. Even at this time the dry fly enthusiast was still in a minority on such rivers as the Wharfe. In his later years he became acquainted with Jim Wynn (1898-1974), of Addingham, who was a well known fly-fisher and a contemporary of T. K. Wilson (Broughton Point) of Skipton. Chippendale, who had many tackle inventions to his credit, speeded up the development of the fixed spool reel invented by Alfred Holden Illingworth also of Otley.

Tom Chippendale was annually engaged to provide trout for the royal party during King George V's annual stay at the Devonshire Arms, Bolton Abbey for the grouse shooting. Chippendale was very secretive about his dressings, claiming that there was something unique in the making of the flies. His pattern book contained many dressings from famous fly-tiers of the Dales and which were obviously personal communications. They included names such as Sylvester Lister, Moon, James Sproats Blades, A. Cawood, Refitt, Bradshaw and Walbran. He produced a manuscript of his dressings; this included water colour paintings of the flies in their actual size. All the dry flies illustrated were on eyed hooks but wet flies where whipped to gut or horsehair. There were specimens of feathers to be used, but it is not certain whether these were Brumfitt's choice or his own.

Harfield H. Edmonds (1883-1956) and Norman Nellis Lee (1881-1951) wrote *Brook and River Trouting* (1916). The two authors were both solicitors in Bradford. The objective of the book was to set down the correct feathers to be used in tying various patterns of North Country trout flies. The list of flies and dressings is thought to be that of Sylvester Lister (1898). Edmonds lived at Embsay Cottage near Skipton-in-Craven, a few miles from the Bolton Abbey water, which he had the privilege of being able to fish. He was an accomplished fly-fisher and regularly took his 20 bag limit. Norman Nellis Lee became joint secretary of the Appletreewick, Barden and Burnsall Angling Club in 1913. He was a greatly respected angler and fly-tyer who passed on his skills to many Wharfedale anglers. He retired from being a solicitor in Bradford and moved to Arncliffe, a small village in Littondale, by the River Skirfare. He is buried in Arncliffe Churchyard next to the River Skirfare.

Harry Newbould, a former Bolton Abbey river keeper was taught fly-tying by Norman Lee. He was an accomplished fly-fisherman and fly-tyer. His son Brian Newbould was also the river keeper at Bolton Abbey. Brian Newbould still ties North Country flies at his father's workbench in an old Dales'cottage. Jim Wynn the keeper on the Farfield Hall stretch of the Wharfe below Bolton Abbey was in regular communication with all the keepers upstream and downstream of the Farfield Hall Stretch.

Timmy Wilson was a frequent visitor to the River Wharfe. He was a fine angler and sportsman, he was also a prolific writer and author and made substantial contributions to the best trout fly-fishing literature. As 'Broughton Point' of the *Yorkshire Post* he was well known in Yorkshire and as T. K. (Timmy) Wilson he was widely known to trout fishermen all over the country. He wrote the monthly angling article in the *Dalesman* magazine. My father, Tom Cross, who also lived in Skipton at one time, knew him well.

There are a number of excellent fly-fishermen who regularly fish the River Wharfe at present. Oliver Edwards is perhaps the best known fly-fisher and fly-dresser who fishes the River Wharfe. His innovative fly dressings have resulted in giving him an international reputation. His recent exploitation of the caseless caddis larvae, *Rhyacophila* and *Hydropsyche*, with his unique tying techniques, has proved most successful for trout and grayling on northern rivers such as the River Wharfe. However, Oliver Edwards still uses the traditional North Country patterns and is most skilful in their use on Dales' rivers.

Carrying on the traditions of their predecessors, it is pleasing to see that the river keepers are maintaining the North Country Style tradition; both Mark Whitehead from Bolton Abbey and Simon Ashworth are both excellent fishermen and fly-tyers. Simon Ashworth's flies are now requested all over the world and his North Country patterns are still true to the original tyings and lethal in the right conditions. Most importantly they are always willing to help anglers new to the water; this is important as their beats cover approximately 12 miles of fishing. The North Country Style continues to thrive under the guidance and expert tuition of various fly-fishermen: John Tyzack, Stuart Minnikin, Jim Curry, Steve Rhodes, Jeff Metcalf, Stuart Crofts, Philip Bailey and Stephen Cheetham to name but a few. Stephen Cheetham continues to tie excellent North Country fly patterns and teaches fly-tying classes at Prince Henry's Grammar School, in Otley. Phil Holding of Cross Hills, North Yorkshire is also a specialist tyer of traditional North Country patterns. Mike Harding the broadcaster and comedian, is also a keen angler and experienced fly-fisherman. Mike Harding has written a book entitled *A Guide to North Country Flies and How to Tie Them* (2009). This book contains some excellent photographs of North Country fly patterns.

Appendices

Appendix 1
Mayflies for the River Wharfe

Leslie Magee in his book *Fly Fishing: The North Country Tradition* (1994), mayflies that are known to be found on the River Wharfe are listed below. The list includes the common name given to the fly, the scientific names, and a list of Jim Wynn's dressings relating to each mayfly. A dressing may have originally intended to represent one particular insect, or several related insects or different families. The list of mayflies for the River Wharfe is based on published and unpublished records from biologists and entomologists and Leslie Magee's own observations. Leslie Magee excluded angler's records and articles within angling journals in compiling the list. The list only includes mayflies and excludes sedges, stoneflies and midge species.

Summer mayfly (*Siphlonurus lacustris*)
Mayfly, Mayfly Half-Spent

Large dark olive (*Baetis rhodani*)
Waterhen Bloa, Greenwell's Glory, Dark Olive Spinner, Ginger Quill, Hackled Red Spinner, Blue Hen Spider, Hackled Olive Dun, Chelker Greenwell, Hackled Early Olive, Little Pheasant Tail, Rough Bodied Poult

Pale watery dun (*Baetis fuscatus (bioculatus)*)
Pale Watery Dun, Little Marriott, Ginger Quill, Grey Duster, Green and Yellow Bloa, Blue Hen Spider, Yellow Dotterel, Tups Indispensable, Yorkshire Tie of Tups, Yellow Snipe, Yellow Poult, Green Quail

Small dark olive (*Baetis scambus*)
Pheasant Tail Spinner, Hackled Red Spinner, Blue Hen Spider, Waterhen Bloa, Rough Bodied Poult, Chelker Greenwell, Hackled Greenwell

Medium olive (*Baetis vernus*)
Greenwell's Glory, Olive Quill, Medium Olive, Pheasant Tail Spinner, Grey Duster, Hackled Red Spinner, Blue Hen Spider, Quill Bodied Coot, Yellow Coot, Blue Dun, Hackled Olive Dun, Yellow Partridge, Little Pheasant Tail, Yellow Snipe, Green Poult

Iron blue (*Baetis muticus (pumilus)*)
Iron Blue Dun, Pheasant Tail Spinner, Blue Hen Spider, Devonshire Blue Upright, Hackled Iron Blue Dun, Copper Partridge, Dark Watchet, Light Watchet, Purple Water Rail, Purple Snipe, Dark Bloa

Blue-winged pale watery amber spinner (*Centroptilum pennulatum*)
Pale Watery Dun, Little Marriott, Ginger Quill, Grey Duster, Green and Yellow Bloa, Yellow Poult

Pale evening dun, Little pale blue, Pale watery dun (*Procloeon bifidum*)
Pale Watery Dun, Little Marriott, Ginger Quill, Grey Duster, Green and Yellow Bloa, Yellow Dotterel

Olive upright, yellow upright (*Rhithrogena semicolorata*)
Light Olive, Yellow Coot, Throstle Wing, Yellow Partridge, Rough Bodied Poult

Yellow may dun (*Heptagenia sulphurea*)
Primrose Dun, Green and Yellow Bloa, Yellow Snipe, Tangerine Partridge

Dark dun, Dusky yellow-streak (*Heptagenia lateralis*)
Yellow Partridge, Dark Drake

Brook dun (*Ecdyonurus torrentis*)
Hackled Red Spinner

March brown (*Ecdyonurus venosus*)
Tangerine Partridge, Winter Brown
August dun, Great red spinner (*Ecdyonurus dispar*)
Great Red Spinner, Hackled Red Spinner, Claret Partridge, Throstle Wing

Ditch dun (*Habrophlebia fusca*)
Dark Drake

Turkey brown (*Paraleptophlebia submarginata*)
Pheasant Tail Spinner

Green drake, Black drake, Grey drake (*Ephemera danica*)
Mayfly, Mayfly Half-spent, Grey Drake

Blue-winged olive, Sherry spinner (*Ephemerella ignita*)
Blue Winged Olive, Blue Winged Olive Spinner, Orange Quill, Pheasant Tail Spinner, Orange Partridge, Rusty Poult, Indian Yellow

Yellow evening dun (*Ephemerella notata*)
Yellow Poult, Rusty Poult, Indian Yellow

Fisherman's curse (*Brachycercus harrisella*), **Angler's curse** (*Caenis macrura, Caenis luctuosa, Caenis robusta, Caenis horaria*)
Fisherman's Curse

Appendix 2
Seasonal calendar for wet flies

Wet Fly Patterns	Jan	Feb	Mar	Apr	May	Jun	Jul	Aug	Sep	Oct	Nov	Dec
Small Ant Fly[G]			◐	◐	◐	◐	●	●	◐	◐		
Green and Yellow Bloa[F]			◐	◐	◐	◐	◐	◐	◐			
A Yorkshire Tie of the Devonshire Blue Upright[G]			◐	●	◐	◐	◐	◐	●	◐		
Blue Hen Spider			◐	◐	◐	◐	◐	◐	◐	◐		
Yellow Coot[G]			●	●	◐	◐	◐	◐	●	●	◐	
Little Pheasant Tail[GS]	◐	◐	◐	◐	◐	◐	◐	◐	◐	◐	◐	◐
Quill Bodied Coot[EG]			◐	◐	●	●	◐	◐	◐	◐		
Yellow Dotterel[G]					◐	●	◐	◐	◐	◐		
February Red[G]		●	●	●	◐	◐	◐					
Smoke Fly[G]				◐	◐	◐	◐	◐	◐	◐	◐	
Gravel Bed Spider			◐	●	◐							
Greansleaves						●	◐					
Fog Black[G]			●	●	◐	◐	◐	●	●	◐	◐	
Hackled Greenwell and Chelker Greenwell[E]					●	●						
Hackled Iron Blue Dun[S]				◐	◐	●	◐	◐				
Claret Landrail[S]					◐	◐	◐	◐	◐			
Grey Drake[E]					●	●						
Skimming Midge[E]						◐	●	●	◐			
Hackled Early Olive[G]		◐	●	◐					◐	◐		
Dark Needle[G]	◐	◐	●	●	◐	◐	◐	●	●	◐	◐	◐
Light Needle[G]	◐	◐	◐	◐	◐	◐	◐	◐	◐	◐	◐	◐
Green Owl						◐	◐	◐				
Copper Partridge[G]		◐	◐	◐	◐	◐	◐	◐	◐	◐	◐	
Orange Partridge[GS]	◐	●	●	●	●	●	◐	◐	◐	●	◐	◐
Claret Partridge[G]			◐	◐				●	●	◐	◐	
Rough Bodied Poult[E]						◐	◐	◐				

Wet Fly Patterns	Jan	Feb	Mar	Apr	May	Jun	Jul	Aug	Sep	Oct	Nov	Dec
Purple Partridge[G]		●	●	◍	◍	◍	◍	◍				
Red Partridge[GS]		●	●	◍	◍	◍	◍					
Tangerine Partridge[GS]			◍	●	●	◍	◍	◍	◍	◍	◍	
Yellow Partridge[S]			◍	●	●	◍	◍	◍	◍	◍		
Green Poult[E]						◍	◍	●	◍			
Rusty Poult[G]						◍	◍	◍	◍	◍		
Yellow Poult				◍	●	◍	◍	◍	◍	◍		
Dark Sedge[ES]					●	●	◍	◍	◍			
Yellow Snipe[G]		●	●	●	◍	◍	◍	◍		●	◍	
Green Quail[E]					◍	●	◍	◍	◍			
Throstle Wing[EG]					◍	●	●	◍	◍	◍	◍	
Purple Water Rail			◍	●	●	◍	◍	◍	◍	◍		
Purple Snipe or Dark Bloa[G]			◍	◍	●	●	◍	◍	◍	●	◍	
A Yorkshire Tie of Tups[E]					◍	●	●	●	◍			
Blue Dun[G]				◍	●	◍	◍	●	●	◍		
Dark Watchet or Iron Blue Dun				◍	●	●	●	●	◍			
Light Watchet[E]				◍	●	●	●	●	◍			
Water Cricket			◍	◍	◍							
Waterhen Bloa[G]			◍	●	●	●	◍	◍	◍	●		
Hackled Olive Dun				●	●	◍	◍	◍	●	●		
Winter Brown[G]		◍	●	●						●	◍	
Hackled Yellow Sally[E]				◍	●	●	◍					
Blue Partridge[S]				●	●	◍	●	◍				

G *Jim Wynn recommended dressing suitable for grayling in addition to brown trout.*
E *Jim Wynn recommended dressing suitable for use in the evening.*
S *Jim Wynn recommended dressing suitable for use after a spate.*
◍ *Good pattern for the month.*
● *Very good pattern for the month.*

Appendix 3
Seasonal calendar for dry flies

Dry Fly Patterns	Jan	Feb	Mar	Apr	May	Jun	Jul	Aug	Sep	Oct	Nov	Dec
Olive Quill					◐	●	●	◐	●	◐		
Greenwell's Glory[F]			◐		●	●	◐	◐	◐	◐		
Medium Olive[E]					●	●	◐	◐				
Light Olive[E]					●	●	●	◐				
Blue Winged Olive[G]					◐	●	◐	◐	◐	◐		
Orange Quill[EG]					◐	●	◐	◐	◐	◐	◐	
Iron Blue Dun (Male)[G]				◐	●	●	◐	◐	●	◐		
Iron Blue Dun (Female)[G]				◐	●	●	◐	◐	●	◐		
Small Red Spinner[E]							◐	●	●	◐		
Dark Olive Spinner	◐	◐	◐	◐	◐					◐	◐	◐
Blue Winged Olive Spinner[EG]					◐	◐	◐	◐	◐	◐		
Pheasant Tail Spinner[G]			◐	◐	◐	◐	◐	◐	◐	◐		
Great Red Spinner			◐	◐	◐	◐	◐	●	●	◐		
Silver Sedge[EG]						◐	●	●	◐	◐		
Pale Watery Dun[G]				◐	●	●	●	◐	◐	◐		
Tups Indispensable[EG]			◐	◐	●	◐	◐					
Badger Midge[EG]			◐	◐	●	●	◐	●	●	◐	◐	
Grey Duster[G]					◐	◐	◐	◐	◐	◐		
Little Mariott Fly[EG]					◐	◐	◐	◐	◐	◐		
Orange Tups[EG]			◐	◐	●	◐	◐	◐	◐	◐		
Ginger Quill[E]			◐	◐	◐	●	●	●	◐	◐		
Orange Sedge[EG]					◐	●	●	◐	◐	◐		
Red Tag	◐	◐	◐	◐	◐	●	●	●	●	●	●	◐
Honey Dun Bumble[G]					◐	◐	◐	◐	●	●		
Naples Yellow Palmer[EG]					◐	◐	◐	◐	◐			
Treacle Parkin[G]	◐	◐	◐	◐	◐	●	●	●	●	●	●	◐

Dry Fly Patterns	Jan	Feb	Mar	Apr	May	Jun	Jul	Aug	Sep	Oct	Nov	Dec
Grey Palmer^G		◍	◍	●	◍	◍	◍	◍	◍	◍	◍	
Red Palmer^EG		◍	◍	◍	◍	●	●	◍	◍	◍		
Mayfly^E					◍	●	●	◍	◍	◍	◍	
Mayfly – half spent^E					◍	●	●	◍				
Fisherman's Curse^E					◍	●	●	●	◍			
Orange Tag^G	◍	◍	◍	◍	◍	●	●	●	●	●	●	◍
Hackled Red Spinner Dry Fly^E							◍	◍	◍	◍		

G *Jim Wynn recommended dressing suitable for grayling in addition to brown trout.*

E *Jim Wynn recommended dressing suitable for use in the evening.*

◍ *Good pattern for the month.*

● *Very good pattern for the month.*

Appendix 4
Jim Wynn's recommended grayling flies for the River Wharfe

Dry flies	*Wet flies*
Iron Bluc Dun	Small Ant Fly
Blue Winged Olive	Quill Bodied Coot
Blue Winged Olive Spinner	Yellow Coot
Pheasant Tail Spinner	A Yorkshire Tie of the Devonshire
Pale Watery Dun	Blue Upright
Orange Quill	Yellow Dotterel
Little Mariott	Blue Dun
Badger Midge	February Red
Tups Indispensable	Fog Black
Orange Tups	Dark Needle
Grey Duster	Light Needle
Silver Sedge	Hackled Early Olive
Orange Sedge	Blue Partridge
Treacle Parkin	Copper Partridge
Orange Tag	Claret Partridge
Red Tag	Orange Partridge
Grey Palmer	Red Partridge
Honey Dun Bumble	Tangerine Partridge
Red Palmer	Rusty Poult
	Smoke Fly
	Throstle Wing
	Little Pheasant Tail
	Purple Snipe
	Yellow Snipe
	Waterhen Bloa
	Purple Water Rail
	Winter Brown

Appendix 5
River Wharfe day ticket fishing

There are a number of stretches of the River Wharfe where day tickets can be purchased, these are listed below.

Arncliffe (River Skirfare) – From Arncliffe you can fish four miles of the River Skirfare. No Sunday fishing. Day tickets can be obtained from the Falcon Inn at Arncliffe (Tel. 01756 770205).

Lower Skirfare to Confluence with the River Wharfe – Kilnsey Angling Club issues day tickets for the lower reaches of the River Skirfare to the confluence with the River Wharfe. Day tickets can be purchased from the Tennants Arms at Kilnsey between 9.30am and 10am (Tel. 01756 752301).

Kilnsey – Kilnsey Angling Club, the second oldest club in the country, have a fine stretch of the River Wharfe that can be fished on a day ticket. Day tickets can be purchased from the Tennants Arms at Kilnsey between 9.30am and 10am (Tel. 01756 752301).

Burnsall – Seven miles of fly fishing upstream of Bolton Abbey water. This stretch is run by Appletreewick, Barden and Burnsall Angling Club. This famous stretch is similar in character to Bolton Abbey. Day tickets can be purchased from the Red Lion in Burnsall (Tel. 01756 720204).

Bolton Abbey – Five miles of double bank brown trout and grayling fishing in spectacular surroundings, controlled by the Chatsworth Estate. This stretch of the River Wharfe offers great fishing and easy accessibility. Tickets can be obtained from the Estate Office in Bolton Abbey (Tel. 01756 718000).

Addingham – The Addingham Angling association has three miles of good fly-fishing for brown trout and grayling throughout the year apart from 15-24 March. The top of this water meets the bottom of the Bolton Abbey water. Day tickets can be purchased from the Post Office, Main Street Addingham (Tel. 01943 830331).

Pool-in-Wharfedale – This stretch of the River Wharfe is controlled by Leeds & District ASA. A day ticket can be purchased which provides 3 miles of fishing upstream and downstream of the road bridge in Pool. Day tickets can be purchased from the petrol station, adjacent to the road bridge at the junction between the A58 and the A659.

References

Aldam, W. H. (1876). *A Quaint Treatise on 'Flees and the Art of Artyfichall Flee Making', by an Old Man.* Day, London.

Austin, R. S. (c. 1890). *Manuscript Book of Dry-Fly Fishing on Exe and other North Devon Streams.* N.d.

Bainbridge, W. G. (1936). *The Fly-Fisher's Guide to Aquatic Flies and Their Imitations.* A. & C. Black Ltd., London.

Bailey, P. (2009). *A Little Book on How to Fish Traditional Hackled Flies.* www.flyfishwithme.net, 2009.

Best, Thomas, (1814). *The Art of Angling.* Crosby & Co., London.

Blacker, W. (1843). *The Art of Fly-Making.* London.

Broughton, R.B. (1989). 'Flies That Catch Grayling' in *Grayling: The Fourth Game Fish*, The Crowood Press, Marlborough.

Bucknall, G. (1994). *To Meet The First March Brown.* Swan Hill Press, London.

Carter Platts, W. (1938). *Modern Trout Fishing.* Adam & Charles Black, London.

Carter Platts, W. (1939). *Grayling Fishing.* Adam & Charles Black, London.

Church, B. and Gathercole, P. (1985). *Imitations of the Trout's World.* The Crowood Press, Marlborough.

Church, B. (1987). *Bob Church's Guide to Trout Flies.* The Crowood Press, Marlborough.

Clarke, B. and Goddard, J. (1980). *The Trout and the Fly.* Ernest Benn Ltd, London.

Collyer, D. J. (1975). *Fly-Dressing.* David and Charles, London.

Courtney Williams, A. (1950). *A Dictionary of Trout Flies.* A. & C. Black, London.

Courtney Williams, A. (1977). *A Dictionary of Trout Flies and Flies for Sea-Trout and Grayling.* Adam and Charles Black, London.

Edmonds, H. H. and Lee, N. N. (1916). *Brook and River Trouting.* (Published privately, Bradford).

Edwards, O. (1994). *Flytyers Masterclass: A step-by-step guide to tying 20 essential flies.* Merlin Unwin Books, Ludlow.

Fogg, W. S. R. (1979). *The Art of the Wet Fly.* A. & C. Black, London.

Fogg, W. S. R. (1988). *A Handbook of North Country Trout Flies.* Old Vicarage Publications, Congleton.

Foster, D. (1886). *The Scientific Angler.* Bemrose.

Francis, F. (1885). *A Book on Angling.* Longmans, Green & Co., London.

Goddard, J. (1976). *Trout Fly Recognition.* Adam and Charles Black, London.

Goddard, J. (1988). *John Goddard's Waterside Guide.* Unwin Hyman, London.

Halford, F.M. (1886). *Floating Flies and How to Dress Them.* Samson, Low, Marston, Searle, and Rivington, London.

Halford, F. M. (1889). *Dry-Fly Fishing in Theory and Practice*. Samson, Low, Marston, Searle, and Rivington, London.

Halford, F. M. (1902). *Dry-Fly Entomology*. Volume II, Vinton, London.

Halford, F. M. (1910). *Modern Development of the Dry Fly*. Routledge, London.

Halford, F. M. (1913). *The Dry-Fly Man's Handbook*. Routledge, London.

Harding, M. (2009). *A Guide to North Country flies and how to tie them*. Aurum Press Ltd, London.

Harris, J. R. (1970). *An Angler's Entomology*. Collins, London.

Hills, J. W. (1921). *A history of fly fishing for trout*. Phillip Allan & Co., London.

Jackson, J. (1854). *The Practical Fly-Fisher*. Farlow, London. Re-published Leeds c. 1880.

Kite, O. (1963). *Nymph Fishing in Practice*. Jenkins, London.

Lawrie, W. H. (1969). *English Trout Flies*. A. S. Barnes and Co, New York.

Leighton, M. (1987). *Trout Flies of Shropshire and the Welsh Borderlands*. Redverse Ltd., Shrewsbury.

McClelland, H. G. (1949). *How to Tie Flies for Trout and Grayling Fishing*. The Fishing Gazette, London.

Magee, L. (1994). *Fly Fishing The North Country Tradition*. Smith Settle, Otley.

Mackintosh, A. (1821). *The Modern Fisher; or, Driffield Angler*, Henry Mozley, Derby.

Mold, F. E. (1967). *Presenting the Fly to the Trout*. Herbert Jenkins, London.

Nelson, W. (1922). *Fishing In Eden*. H. F. & G. Witherby, London.

Nemes, S. (1975). *The Soft-Hackled Fly*. Chatam Press.

Nemes, S. (1981). *The Soft-Hackled Fly Addict*. Published privately in the United States.

O'Reilly, P. (1990). *Tactical Fly Fishing*. The Crowood Press, Marlborough.

O'Reilly, P. (2003). *Matching the Hatch: Stillwater, River & Stream*. Swan Hill Press, Shrewsbury.

Overfield, T. D. (1972). *Famous Flies and Their Originators*. Adam and Charles Black, London.

Overfield, T. D. (1980). *Fifty Favourite Dry Flies*. Ernest Benn Limited, London.

Overfield, T. D. (1986). *Fifty Favourite Wet Flies*. A. & C. Black, London.

Parsons, J. (1988). *Deceiving Trout The Flytier's Art*. Airlife, Shrewsbury.

Proper, D. (1993). *What the Trout Said*. Swan Hill Press, Shrewsbury.

Price, S. D. (1976). *Rough Stream Trout Flies*. Adam and Charles Black, London.

Pritt, T. E. (1885). *Yorkshire Trout Flies*. Goodall and Siddick, Leeds.

Pritt, T. E. (1886). *North Country Flies*. Sampson, Low, Marston, Searle and Rivington, London.

Pritt, T. E. (1896). *The Book of the Grayling*. Privately published, Leeds.

Ransome, A. (1980). *Rod and Line*. Oxford University Press, Oxford.

Righyni, R. V. (1968). *Grayling*. MacDonald, London.

Roberts, J. (1988). *To Rise a Trout*. The Crowood Press, Marlborough.

Robert, J. (1989). *A Guide to River Trout Flies*. The Crowood Press, Marlborough.

Roberts, J. (1988). *The New Dictionary of Trout Flies*. Unwin Hyman Limited, London.

Roberts, J. (1995). *Illustrated Dictionary of Trout Flies*. Collins Willow, London.

Rolt, H. A. (1901). *Grayling Fishing in South Country Streams*. Sampson, Low, Marston and Co, London.

Ronalds, A. (1836). *The Fly-Fisher's Entomology*. Longman, Brown, Green and Longman, London.

Saville, T. (1991). *Reservoir Trout Fishing with Tom Saville*. H. F. and G. Witherby Ltd., London.

Sawyer, F. (1970). *Nymphs and the Trout*. A. & C. Black, London.

Shipley, W. (1838). *Fly Fishing*. Edited by Edward Fitzgibbon. Simpkin, Marshall & Co, London.

Skues, G. E. M. (1910). *Minor Tactics of the Chalk Stream*. A. & C. Black, London.

Skues, G. E. M. (1921). *The Way of the Trout with a Fly*. A. & C. Black, London.

Skues, G. E. M. (1928). *The Way of a Trout with a Fly*. A. & C. Black, London.

Skues, G. E. M. (1939). *Nymph Fishing for Chalk Stream Trout*. A. & C. Black, London.

Stewart, T. (1964). *Fifty Popular Flies and How to Tie Them. Volume 1*. E. M. Art & Publishing Ltd., Peterborough.

Stewart, T. (1964). *Fifty Popular Flies and How to Tie Them. Volume 2*. E. M. Art & Publishing Ltd., Peterborough.

Stewart, T. (1969). *Fifty Popular Flies and How to Tie Them. Volume 3*. Ernest Benn Limited., London.

Stewart, T. (1973). *Two Hundred Popular Flies And How To Tie Them*. Ernest Benn Limited, London.

Swarbrick, J. and Sagar, J. W. (1907). *List of Wharfedale Flies by John Swarbrick (of Austby)*, 1807 and J. W. Sagar, 1890. Copyright E. Beanlands. Printed by Helmsley & Sons, Ilkley.

Theakson, M. (1853). *British Angling Flies*. Revised and annotated by Francis Walbran, Low, Ripon.

Tod, E. M. (1903). *Wet-Fly Fishing*. Sampson Low, Marston and Co., London.

Townsend, D. C. (1980). *Fly-Tying with Harold Howarth*. Adam and Charles Black, London.

Turton, J. (1836). *The Angler's Manual*. R. Groombridge, London.

Veniard, J. (1964). *Fly Dressers' Guide*. Fifth Impression. A. & C. Black Ltd., London.

Walbran, F. M. (1889). *Walbran's British Angler*. Simpkin, Marshall and Co.

Walbran, F. M. (1895). *Grayling and how to catch them*. Privately published.

Walker, C. F. (1953). *Chalk Stream Flies*. A. & C. Black, London.

Walker, C. F. (1957). *Fly-Tying as an Art*. Herbert Jenkins, London.

Walker, R. (1974). *Fly Dressing Innovations*. Benn, Tonbridge.

Walton, I. and Cotton, C. (1891). *The Compleat Angler*. Edited by George W. Bethune, London.

Wilson, T. K. (1966). *Trout by all means*. E. M. Art and Publishing, Peterborough.

Woolley, R. (1932). *Modern Trout Fly Dressing*. The Fishing Gazette, London.

Woolley, R. (1938). *The Fly-Fisher's Flies*. The Fishing Gazette, London.

Manuscripts and fly lists relevant to the River Wharfe

This list of manuscripts is from Leslie Magee's book *Fly Fishing: The North Country Tradition*, 1994, Smith Settle, Otley. The reader should refer to this book for more details about the flies included in these manuscripts and lists.

Brumfitt, William (1872). *Manuscript Book of North Country Patterns for Trout and Grayling*. William Brumfitt, Otley. (with later editions by Tom Chippendale of Otley. n.d.). Some of the illustrations for Pritt's *Yorkshire Trout Flies* were engraved from the water colour illustration in this manuscript, as well as from flies tied by Brumfitt.

Emmott, Joseph (1900). *Trout and Grayling Flies*. Joseph Emmott of Ilkley. List of 30 flies supplied by J. Emmott (Fly-Tyer), son of Jerome Emmott, keeper of the Kilnsey Angling Club, who tied some of the flies for Pritt's *Yorkshire Trout Flies*. The list gives the seasons.

Lister, Sylvester, (1898). *List of Artificial Flies used by Sylvester Lister Snr. Barden Tower, Nr Bolton Abbey*. The original manuscript is on parchment and was dictated to Sylvester's daughter-in-law, Mrs Boothman, two years before his death. (The handwriting has been verified). Lister had fished the Wharfe for 60 years. The manuscript formed the basis of Edmonds and Lee's list of 1916.

Pickard, John (1820). *List of Flies for River Wharfe*. John Pickard of Bramham Hall, Yorkshire. Mainly copied from John Swarbrick's list of 1807, but includes several patterns not in Beanland's copy.

Pilling, William (1794). *List of Artificial Flies for ye River Wharfe*. William Pilling, Miller, of Pool-in-Wharfedale, (Abraham Huddleston's List).

Swarbrick, John (1807). *List of Wharfedale Flies*. John Swarbrick of Austby. (A manuscript dated 1818 was at one time in possession of Carter Platts, text slightly different). E. Beanlands copy was published by Helmsley & Sons, Ilkley, 1907. E. Beanlands was a close friend of Carter Platts.

Sagar, J.W. (1890). *List of Wharfedale Flies*. Published by E. Beanlands. Printed by Helmsley & Sons, Ilkley, 1907.

Walbran, F. M. (1896 c.). *Walbran's Fly Wallet*. Francis Walbran. The wallet contains the names of the flies and the seasons for their use as well as hundreds of North Country artificial flies tied to gut. There are fine unused specimens of Sea-swallow, Dotterel and Brown Owl.

Walbran, F. M. (1900-1909). *Walbran Manuscripts*. Walbran, F. M. Manuscripts and notes compiled by F. M. Walbran between 1900-1909. Some items previously published; some appear to have been intended for an autobiography.